Vernacular Architecture

John M. Coggeshall
and
Jo Anne Nast

Southern Illinois University Press

in Southern Illinois

The Ethnic Heritage

Photographs by Randy Tindall

Carbondale and Edwardsville

Copyright © 1988 by the Board of Trustees
Southern Illinois University
All rights reserved
Printed in the United States of America
Edited by Carol J. Pierman
Design and production by Natalia Nadraga

91 90 89 88   4 3 2 1

Library of Congress Cataloging-in-Publication Data
Coggeshall, John M.
  Vernacular architecture in southern Illinois.
  (Shawnee books)
  1. Ethnic architecture—Illinois. 2. Vernacular
architecture—Illinois. I. Nast, Jo Anne.
II. Tindall, Randy. III. Title.
NA730.I3C64   1988   720'.9773   87-26448
ISBN 0-8093-1462-2
ISBN 0-8093-1463-0 (pbk.)

The paper used in this publication meets the minimum requirements of American National Standard for Information Sciences—Permanence of Paper for Printed Library Materials, ANSI Z39.48-1984. ♾™

Contents

Plates   vii

Acknowledgments   xiii

1. Introduction   3

2. The French   11

3. The Anglo-Americans   33

4. The Germans   69

5. The Poles   111

6. The Italians   135

7. The Slovakians   161

8. Eclectic Influences   183

Plates

2. The French

2.1. Site of Village of Kaskaskia   15
2.2. Kaskaskia-Cahokia Trail, Chester Vicinity   16
2.3. Prairie du Rocher Vicinity   17
2.4. Prairie du Rocher Vicinity   18
2.5. Menard House, Ellis Grove Vicinity   19
2.6. Menard House, Ellis Grove Vicinity   19
2.7. Creole House, Prairie du Rocher   20
2.8. View from Creole House, Prairie du Rocher   21
2.9. Cletus Pierre Menard Community Building, Prairie du Rocher   22
2.10. Johnson Cabin, Prairie du Rocher   23
2.11. Rear, Johnson Cabin, Prairie du Rocher   23
2.12. Rear Wall Detail, Johnson Cabin, Prairie du Rocher   24
2.13. Chinking, Johnson Cabin, Prairie du Rocher   25
2.14. Stone Silo, Prairie du Rocher   26
2.15. Robert's Store, Prairie du Rocher   27
2.16. Tombstone, St. Joseph Cemetery, Prairie du Rocher   28
2.17. Cabin, Modoc Vicinity   29
2.18. Detail of North Wall, Cabin, Modoc Vicinity   30
2.19. Fults House, Fults Vicinity   31
2.20. Cabin, Grand Tower Vicinity   32

3. The Anglo-Americans

3.1. Kaskaskia-Cahokia Trail, Waterloo Vicinity   37
3.2. Bellefontaine Site, Waterloo Vicinity   38
3.3. Bellefontaine Spring, Waterloo Vicinity   39
3.4. James Moore Cabin, Waterloo Vicinity   40
3.5. Moore House, Waterloo Vicinity   41
3.6. McRoberts House, Maeystown Vicinity   42
3.7. Notching Detail, Log Cabin, Waterloo   43
3.8. William Biggs Cabin, Waterloo   44
3.9. Peterstown House, Waterloo   46
3.10. Panorama, Golconda   47

3.11. Panorama, Golconda   48
3.12. Panorama, Golconda   48
3.13. First Presbyterian Church, Golconda   50
3.14. Richard Taylor House, Golconda   51
3.15. Downtown View, Elizabethtown   52
3.16. Rose Hotel, Elizabethtown   53
3.17. Lightner House, Elizabethtown   54
3.18. Davis Log Cabin, Herod   55
3.19. Cabin, Eichorn Vicinity   57
3.20. St. Patrick's Roman Catholic Church, Cairo   58
3.21. Front Entryway, St. Patrick's Roman Catholic Church, Cairo   59
3.22. Landscape, Cobden Vicinity   60
3.23. Bailey House, Jonesboro   61
3.24. Coomes House, Jonesboro   62
3.25. St. Ann's Episcopal Church, Anna   63
3.26. Double Pen House, Macedonia   64
3.27. Log Barn, Piopolis   65
3.28. Notching Detail, Log Cabin, Piopolis   66
3.29. Pegging Detail, Log Cabin, Piopolis   67

4. The Germans

4.1. Hanover Street, Maeystown   73
4.2. Bundy Farm, Maeystown   74
4.3. Springhouse, Waterloo Vicinity   75
4.4. Springhouse Interior, Waterloo Vicinity   76
4.5. Outdoor Bake Oven, Waterloo Vicinity   77
4.6. Platz House, Columbia Vicinity   78
4.7. Cellar, Werling House, Waterloo Vicinity   79
4.8. Front Door, Buss House, Waterloo Vicinity   80
4.9. Detail of Sandstone Lintel, Buss House, Waterloo Vicinity   81
4.10. Gundlach-Grosse House, Columbia   82
4.11. Structural Detail, Hartmann Barn, Waterloo Vicinity   83
4.12. Summer Kitchen, "Stonewood," Columbia Vicinity   84
4.13. Barn Door, "Stonewood," Columbia Vicinity   85
4.14. Barn Window, "Stonewood," Columbia Vicinity   86
4.15. Mueller Barn, Maeystown Vicinity   88
4.16. Mueller Barn, Maeystown Vicinity   89
4.17. Salem-Baum Evangelical Church, Maeystown Vicinity   90
4.18. Steeple, St. Paul's United Church of Christ, Waterloo   91
4.19. Brinkmann House, Waterloo Vicinity   92
4.20. Deerhaake House, Germantown Vicinity   93
4.21. St. Boniface Roman Catholic Church, Germantown   94
4.22. Interior of Belltower, St. Boniface Roman Catholic Church, Germantown   95

4.23. Tombstone, St. Boniface Roman Catholic Cemetery, Germantown   96
4.24. Station of the Cross, St. Boniface Roman Catholic Cemetery, Germantown   97
4.25. Linnemann House, Germantown   98
4.26. Bartelso Vicinity   99
4.27. Interior, St. Cecilia's Roman Catholic Church, Bartelso   100
4.28. Jantzen's Store, Bartelso   101
4.29. Paul Wellen House, Piopolis   102
4.30. George Stich House, Piopolis   103
4.31. Herzing House, Piopolis   104
4.32. Rubenacher Barn, Piopolis   106
4.33. Humm-Pairsh House, Elizabethtown   107
4.34. Gable Detail, Cano House, Grand Tower   108

5. The Poles

5.1. Main Street, DuBois   115
5.2. Nikrant Barn, DuBois Vicinity   116
5.3. Nikrant Barn, DuBois Vicinity   117
5.4. Kuhn Hardware Store, DuBois   118
5.5. Kuhn House, DuBois   119
5.6. St. Charles Borromeo Roman Catholic Church, DuBois   120
5.7. St. Charles Borromeo Roman Catholic Church, DuBois   121
5.8. Holy Scapular Society, DuBois   122
5.9. St. Mark's United Church of Christ and St. Charles Borromeo Roman Catholic Church (background), DuBois   123
5.10. Ksycki Store, DuBois   124
5.11. Ksycki Store, DuBois   125
5.12. Chapel Hill School, DuBois Vicinity   126
5.13. Main Thoroughfare, Radom   127
5.14. Szopinski Store, Radom   128
5.15. Crucifixion Shrine, St. Michael's Roman Catholic Cemetery, Radom Vicinity   129
5.16. Monument, St. Michael's Roman Catholic Cemetery, Radom Vicinity   130
5.17. Station of the Cross, St. Michael's Roman Catholic Church, Radom   131
5.18. Main Thoroughfare, Posen   132

6. The Italians

6.1. Northeast Commercial District, Herrin   139
6.2. Rome Club, Herrin   140
6.3. Rome Club, Herrin   141
6.4. Main Entrance, Rome Club, Herrin   142
6.5. Our Lady of Mt. Carmel Roman Catholic Church, Herrin   145
6.6. Our Lady of Mt. Carmel Roman Catholic Church, Herrin   146

Plates

6.7. Tombstone, San Carlo Roman Catholic Cemetery, Herrin   147
6.8. C. C. Club Bar, Herrin   148
6.9. Ballroom Interior Detail, C. C. Club, Herrin   149
6.10. Detail of Stairs to Ballroom, C. C. Club, Herrin   150
6.11. Ballroom, C. C. Club, Herrin   151
6.12. Detail of Ballroom Ceiling, C. C. Club, Herrin   152
6.13. Ballroom Bandstand, C. C. Club, Herrin   153
6.14. Town Bakery, Herrin   154
6.15. Display Window, Town Bakery, Herrin   155
6.16. Detail of Facade, Dell'Era Building, Herrin   156
6.17. Northside Neighborhood, Herrin   158
6.18. Grape Arbor, "Lombardy Neighborhood," Herrin   159

7. The Slovakians

7.1. Protection of the Virgin Mary Orthodox Church, Royalton   165
7.2. Protection of the Virgin Mary Orthodox Church, Royalton   166
7.3. Dedicatory Monument, Protection of the Virgin Mary Orthodox Church, Royalton   168
7.4. Interior, Protection of the Virgin Mary Orthodox Church, Royalton   169
7.5. Orthodox Christian Cemetery, Royalton Vicinity   170
7.6. Tombstone, Orthodox Christian Cemetery, Royalton Vicinity   171
7.7. United Mine Workers of America Union Hall, Royalton   172
7.8. United Mine Workers of America Union Hall, Royalton   173
7.9. Main Thoroughfare, Royalton   174
7.10. Dowell Mining Company Store, Dowell   175
7.11. Private Home, Dowell   176
7.12. Private Home, Dowell   177
7.13. Azeling House, Royalton   178
7.14. Orthodox Chapel, Dowell   179
7.15. Company Houses, Colp Vicinity   180

8. Eclectic Influences

8.1. Hamilton House, Murphysboro   186
8.2. Halliday House, Cairo   188
8.3. Steyer-Billington House, Golconda   189
8.4. Sloan House, Golconda   190
8.5. Stone Outbuilding, Sloan House, Golconda   191
8.6. Cloud State Bank and McCoy Memorial Library, McLeansboro   192
8.7. Residence, Golconda   193
8.8. Nelson House, Grand Tower   194
8.9. Christen Rubenacher House, Piopolis   195
8.10. Lohr Bottling Company, Cairo   196

8.11. Spalt's Barn, Cobden   197
8.12. Warner Wall House, Mound City   198
8.13. Tin Store Fronts, Mounds   199
8.14. Downtown Businesses, Cairo   200
8.15. Barn and Silos, Benton Vicinity   201
8.16. Shotgun Houses, Cairo   202
8.17. Shotgun Houses, Mounds   203

Acknowledgments

This book represents the final stage of a project originally sponsored by the University Museum, Southern Illinois University, Carbondale. The research and exhibition phases of this project, "The Architectural History of Southern Illinois," were supported in large part through grants provided by the Illinois Humanities Council and the National Endowment for the Humanities.

Funds for the publication of the project were provided through the generous donations of the University Museum Associates under the leadership of the 1986–87 president, Dr. Robert Jensen. Their support has made possible the publication of this volume.

This project could not have been administered and maintained without the assistance and support of each member of the museum staff. In particular Dr. John J. Whitlock, the director, has supported the project from its inception and has participated in many roles, from fiscal officer to reviewer of the final manuscript. Special recognition is also extended to the museum's exhibit designer, Alan Harasimowicz, who designed and, with his staff, installed the exhibition; to graduate assistant, Lillian Maring, who provided invaluable assistance in conducting research, coordinating photos, and attending to innumerable details in the preparation of the publication manuscript; and to graduate assistants, Mark Tang, who painstakingly printed the exhibition photos, and Debra Wimmer, who provided research assistance in the fieldwork phase of the project.

Additional support in the form of telephones, stationery, wordprocessing facilities, secretarial help, and office space came from the Department of Anthropology at Southern Illinois University, the Department of Sociology and Anthropology at Radford University, Radford, Virginia, and the Department of Sociology, Clemson University, Clemson, South Carolina. Thanks to them as well.

To the faithful band of tape transcribers we are also grateful. They patiently transcribed the field tapes, often recorded under very trying conditions. All this was accomplished in addition to their regular duties for the University Museum.

A number of professional humanists acting as consultants and evaluators, have been involved in the supervision of this project, and each of them is commended for offering valuable time and expertise to ensure its quality. Two participants in particular deserve special recognition: first, R. Gail White, AIA, of White and Borgognoni Architects P.C., Carbondale, assisted the fieldworkers and museum staff in identifying communities for study, helped define the scope of the research, shared his research files and publications, and answered innumerable questions without complaint; second, Kelly Cichy, Research Development Coordinator, Graduate Studies and Research, University of Massachusetts, Boston, Research Development and Administration, Southern Illinois University, Carbondale, conducted the field research for the initial survey phase of the project in fall 1985 with John M. Coggeshall.

A sincere debt of gratitude is extended to each of the informants, building owners and homeowners, and local historians who welcomed the researchers into their communities, and indeed their homes, and provided the information upon which the primary research was founded. Although hundreds of southern Illinoisans have participated in this project, special thanks is extended to the following individuals who took the lead in their communities and assisted the researchers in locating informants, sites, and historical data: Mary Ksycki, DuBois; Al Hartman, Waterloo; Louise Ogg, Cairo; Mabel Stannard and the Pope County Historical Society, Golconda; Reverend Mark Stevens, Royalton; Angelo and Theresa Calcaterra, Herrin; Reverend James Calhoun, Germantown; Charles Frey, Anna; and Mike Jones, Murphysboro.

Special recognition is due to Guy Gordon Weaver, coresearcher, assistant photographer, and coauthor on the project. His talent and professionalism is reflected throughout the pages of this book. And, most importantly, sincere thanks are due to Randy Tindall, project photographer. Without his steady hand and keen eye the photographs would have been merely documentary and not artistic as well. Randy captured many scenes only with extreme difficulty but met each challenge with calm perseverance. Without Randy's tireless professionalism and skillful expertise, the book would not have been possible.

From the very beginning the production of this book has been a collaborative effort. Because of parallel anthropological and folkloristic training and interests, both authors share the same general perspective on ethnic and vernacular architecture and its relationship to culture. The book expresses this combined view. Nevertheless, we feel it necessary to credit the work of each author as well, in order to distinguish specific views and to respect each other's contributions. Jo Anne Nast wrote the overview of the project, while John M. Coggeshall added the section on ethnic cultural modifications to the landscape. Most of the captions for the Anglo-American chapter were written by Nast, while Coggeshall submitted those from southwestern Illinois and wrote the chapter text. Text and captions for chapter 2 and those for chapters 4 through 7 were written by Coggeshall; Nast contributed the text and captions for chapter 8 and edited the overall work.

Vernacular Architecture
in Southern Illinois

1. Introduction

This book derives from a two-phase project, originally titled "The Architectural History of Southern Illinois," that focused on ethnic influences on the built environment, specifically vernacular architecture. In the wider scope, the built environment, which we refer to as "ethnic architecture," includes domestic, commercial, and ecclesiastical building styles, the cultural use of space, place names, epigraphic and related inscriptions, settlement patterns, and some types of folk art and material culture.

The first phase of the project, conducted in fall 1985, provided funds for two researchers to conduct a four-week field survey to identify communities in which ethnic influences were strong. This survey documented the influence of seven distinct ethnic groups in over twenty-two communities; these groups included the French, Anglo-American, German, Polish, Slovakian, Italian, and black American.

In the second phase of the project, a nine-week field session was conducted to investigate these communities in greater depth and to narrow the focus of the research to approximately fifteen of these communities. A team of three professional humanists with field research experience was hired to conduct this phase of the project. The team consisted of Dr. John M. Coggeshall, with the Department of Anthropology, Southern Illinois University, Carbondale, Illinois, and Guy Gordon Weaver and Randy Tindall, Ph.D. candidates in the Department of Anthropology, Southern Illinois University, Carbondale.

Fieldwork consisted of oral historical interviews and photo documentation of buildings important to the ethnic community. The research had three goals: to pinpoint specific examples of ethnic architecture in each community; to gain a wider perception of general ethnic cultural modifications to the landscape; and to enhance the photographs by obtaining firsthand information about each ethnic group. In addition to merely photographing buildings and landscapes, the research verified the cultural importance of these modifications for each group.

In nine weeks, preliminary research was conducted on the influence of seven ethnic groups in over fifteen southern Illinois communities, including Prairie du Rocher, Maeystown, Waterloo, Bartelso, Germantown, Piopolis, Herrin, DuBois, Radom, Posen, Royalton, Grand Tower, Elizabethtown, Golconda, and Cairo. A limited amount of research was conducted in Modoc, Colp, Dowell, Columbia, Anna, Jonesboro, Cobden, Mound City, and Mounds. The research data collected were in turn used to mount a major photographic exhibition at the University Museum, "The Architectural History of Southern Illinois," which opened November 1986 and remained on display through December 1987.

The research and photographs presented in this publication are the result of the two initial phases of the "Architectural History of Southern Illinois" project.

The goal of the project was to research and document ethnic influences upon vernacular architecture. The research focus was twofold and required an understanding of both

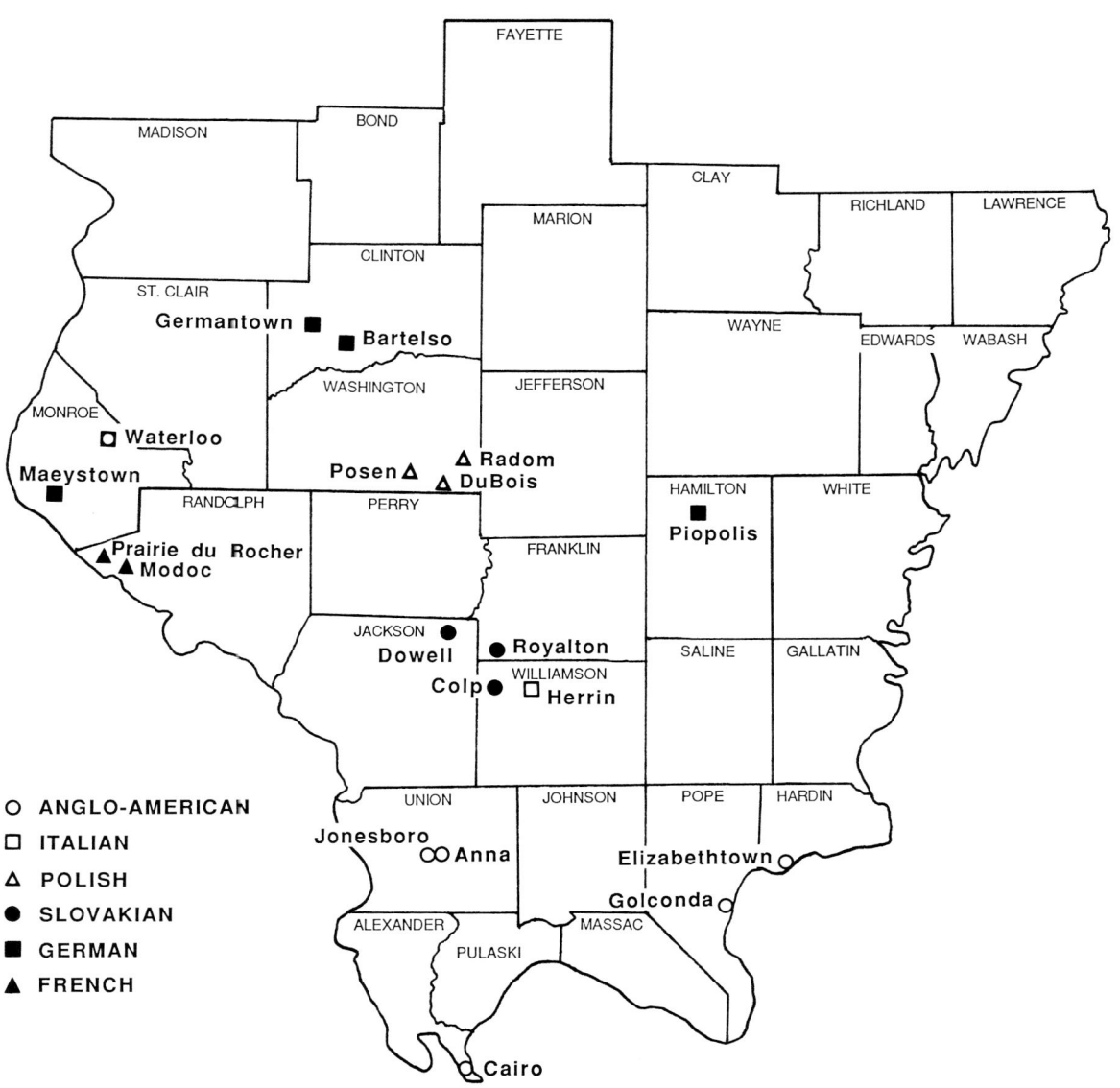

Communities investigated during summer 1986.

ethnic studies with regard to building traditions as well as that of vernacular architecture—both relatively new fields of investigation.

The study of vernacular architecture has, in the last ten to fifteen years, gained considerable attention, particularly among cultural geographers, historical archaeologists, and social historians, as well as among the general public interested in historic preservation issues. Many definitions have been proposed for vernacular architecture, but all share several key elements. Vernacular architecture is characterized by the following: (1) common, everyday structures; (2) structures built without the aid of an architect; (3) forms dictated by function; and (4) construction, for the most part, from locally available materials.

Folklorists have long studied ethnicity, the shared cultural patterns that unite a group; however, emphasis has been placed on the persistence and change within such groups of traits such as customs, language, arts, and material culture traditions. However, the study of common housing or what folklorists term "folk" or "traditional" architecture, and the study of ethnic building traditions, is still relatively new.

Traditionally, formal studies of American architecture have focused on the development of high style architecture, particularly in New England and along the East Coast, such as the early Georgian styles of the eighteenth century, the proliferation in the latter half of the nineteenth century of styles such as Victorian, Queen Anne, Romanesque, and stylistic mixtures. Very little attention had been paid to "common" housing and its development and role in American culture. And yet, in the introduction to one of the first major publications on American vernacular architecture, *Common Places: Readings in American Vernacular Architecture*, Dell Upton and John Michael Vlach cite a study which revealed that only about 5 percent of the world's built environment is designed and constructed by professional architects and engineers.

Historic preservationists, in both rural and urban areas, have brought to public attention the importance of preserving the cultural landscape and the need for conserving both high style and vernacular architecture. Through urban renewal, adaptive reuse, and neighborhood revivals, domestic and public vernacular architecture is being documented and saved as part of America's historical and architectural heritage.

Nevertheless, the study of vernacular architecture is still in its early development. And while some areas of the United States have been studied closely, particularly Virginia, New England, and Pennsylvania, most areas of the United States have not been studied in depth. Southern Illinois is one of these areas. Some scholarly work has been conducted in the region with regard to diffusion of Upland South housing types. Other than these studies, however, only general surveys of historical structures, or studies of particular types of structures, such as barns or churches, have been conducted. With the exception of German influences upon domestic residences in St. Clair County, little investigation of the variety of housing types extant in southern Illinois and the ethnic influence upon such structures had been conducted prior to the Museum's project.

One overriding problem in conducting such research and securing outside funding for such a project, on both the state and federal level, is the generally held view that southern Illinois is essentially comprised of an Upland South, Anglo-American population. It is the goal of this and subsequent studies to temper this view and to draw attention to the rich ethnic diversity of the area.

Southern Illinois is noted for its rugged, natural beauty. As each immigrant group settled the land, it modified the landscape to suit its cultural perceptions of reality. In short, each group remodeled its environment to make it "look right," using contemporary vernacular styles deemed appropriate. Since each group had different cultural traditions, the area developed layers of tradition, as each succeeding group built upon and modified styles of preceding groups. Revealing the layers of vernacular architectural styles and relating these directly to the cultural heritage of each ethnic group is the focus of the book.

Ethnic architecture refers to the modification of space to fit the cultural perceptions of a particular group. Culture, as a set of mental rules, organizes perceptions of reality and suggests proper ways for social interaction. Cultural rules also influence the material ways groups shape their world. Culture provides a framework, a mental pattern; individuals modify their environment to fit the pattern as closely as possible. This transformation includes a diversity of alternatives: perceptions of proper living and work environments; adjustments for climate and topography; proximity to neighbors or livestock; conceptions of appropriate building materials and technology; as well as a desire to continue traditions and patterns from earlier generations.

However, ethnic groups rarely have a completely free hand in modifying the environment to suit their cultural perceptions. Such factors as climate and topography, for example, limit choices of building materials or of homesites. The location of other groups, whether longtime residents or recent immigrants, also may affect where a group settles and why it chooses to live there. Xenophobia may prohibit or inhibit neighborhood assimilation, and continued antagonism may prevent or curtail physical expressions of nonnative cultural traditions. Access to roads, railroads, and markets might restrict or increase the types and cost of construction materials for homes, businesses, and outbuildings. Finally, the acceptance of popular national or regional architectural styles, that is, the desire to live in a "modern" home, also influences ethnic architectural patterns.

Ethnic architecture thus combines past cultural traditions with contemporary limitations, vernacular, "folk" or "traditional" constructions with popular and high styles. Specifically, ethnic architecture includes the cultural use of space; settlement patterns; domestic, commercial, and ecclesiastical building styles; place names; epigraphic and related inscriptions; and some types of folk art and material culture. Numerous examples of these exist in southern Illinois. Many will be examined in detail, exploring the complex relationship between a group's cultural traditions and the environment in which they settled. The combinations and permutations of architectural styles and ethnic heritage, combined with the limitations of prevailing physical environment and previous cultural groups, have woven a complex tapestry on the loom of the southern Illinois landscape. The book examines the warp and weft of this tapestry, as well as the weaving process itself.

In effect, ethnic architecture becomes a physical expression of a group's cultural perceptions of itself and its relationship to other groups. Thus the book concentrates on vernacular styles significant to the groups themselves. Only by examining ethnic architecture from the perspective of the group can one observe how and why these styles and structures reveal the cultural heritage and current expression of a group's identity. For example, numerous residents in several towns representing three different ethnic backgrounds specifically related the Greek Revival architectural style to the German-American ethnic group. To many local residents, a German house is characterized by a small brick home, often a duplex, sitting squarely on the street. Outsiders, though, perceive no logical or necessary relationship between a German house type and the Greek Revival style, although the style's popularity may have peaked in association with German immigration to the area. For whatever reason, brick homes with parallel features were viewed historically, and still are defined, as "typically German" by local residents. Moreover, the neat orderliness of the style's classical lines, as well as the large backyards for garden space, tie directly to perceived cultural attributes of Germans, both in the past and present. The Greek Revival style has become an outward expression of group identity, a physical symbol of past and present cultural traditions. A group need not physically transform southern Illinois into replicas of Old World communities in order to express its ethnic identity; identity may be expressed in less direct ways as well. A row of small houses built right on the street may not necessarily be German to outsiders, but it "looks German" to the observing groups.

Within these pages are photographs of dozens of examples of physical expressions of a group's identity: churches, stores, taverns, private homes, barns, and outbuildings. Each is significant, not for the beauty of the building itself, but because that particular building means something to a particular ethnic group. Since vernacular architectural styles reflect ethnic cultural patterns, then these patterns are reinforced by the buildings themselves. The buildings become concrete expressions and manifestations of cultural identity. One cannot record only the structures and infer their meaning; to bring them alive, the ethnic group for whom the buildings and styles are indicative must explain why this is so.

For example, the C. C. Club in Herrin, to an outsider, seems to be just another tavern, a cool, dark place to while away a humid summer afternoon. But, to Herrin's Lombard Italian-Americans, the C. C. Club professes a symbolic importance. The building represents a direct tie to the Old Country and a place where immigrants, their sons, and grandsons once congregated to tell stories, sing songs, and share a drink in camaraderie.

Outsiders cannot hear the voices; the following pages attempt to recapture them through both words and photographs.

The book does not document classic or idealized architectural styles or the homes of illustrious or wealthy individuals. Instead, the book depicts the styles of the folk, the ordinary people who cleared the fields, raised the children, built the railroads, mined the coal, and manufactured the goods that literally shaped southern Illinois. The styles, traditions, and buildings illustrated within are those important to them, not necessarily to outsiders or to academics. The following pages examine ethnic architecture from the groups' own perspectives, explaining often in their own words why buildings, styles, and traditions remain significant to them.

The French and Anglo-Americans colonized the area, blazing trails and founding settlements. The Germans built upon this foundation, modifying towns or constructing new ones according to their own cultural traditions. The Poles, Italians, and Slovakians provided the muscle for the area's industrial and agricultural expansion, constructing railroads, mining coal, and producing crops. While doing so, they contributed additional modifications to suit their own cultural perceptions. Each group has contributed both physically and culturally, in its own unique way, to the shaping of the southern Illinois landscape. Today, one may still read these cultural modifications to the landscape as layers of tradition, physically reflecting the cultural persistence of these groups in southern Illinois.

This book, the result of one nine-week field season, must be considered a preliminary to a longer, more comprehensive study. Again and again, overwhelming cooperation from residents increased geometrically the amount of material to examine, despite a rapidly diminishing amount of time in which to do so. In effect, only a tiny sample of extant vernacular architecture and related ethnic traditions from southern Illinois has been surveyed. There was always a "bigger one that got away": a more articulate or informed resident, a more exemplary or picturesque building, an older or more indicative community. Even the number of architectural photographs and cultural information had to be edited to meet spatial and financial reality. A project lasting a year or more might be sufficient to blanket southern Illinois communities with an army of interviewers, photographers, and historians; then the complete story might be documented. Much more lies out there, and action is needed to preserve crumbling buildings and record fading memories before time erases them forever.

Nevertheless, the interest generated by this research can be channeled into positive action. Researchers and residents may elaborate upon the original study to explore groups and communities overlooked here. In effect, consider the book not the final chapter on the vernacular architecture of ethnic groups in southern Illinois, but only the opening paragraph.

2. The French

Chronologically, the French are the oldest permanent European group to settle in Illinois. Seeking to establish a commercial empire in the heart of America, the French constructed forts and blazed trails to protect their economic and military investment. Settlers arrived from France and French-speaking Canada, founding small communities near the forts or along the trails. For example, French-speaking immigrants, black slaves and freed people, and native American allies founded the first settlement of Prairie du Rocher about 1722. A typical French colonial town, it lay at the foot of the Mississippi bluffs, near Fort de Chartres, and along the vital overland route linking the more significant French communities of Kaskaskia to the south and Cahokia to the north. French immigration largely declined after the American Revolution, but Prairie du Rocher retained its French heritage. Today, over two hundred years later, the community still displays the physical and cultural imprint of the French.

Upon their arrival, the French restructured their environment to meet their cultural perceptions. The village itself was situated on the Mississippi floodplain because rivers served as principal highways for French commercial interests. The Kaskaskia-Cahokia Trail through Prairie du Rocher connected residents with those French settlements, creating a French corridor in Illinois. In the village, residents reserved a village commons and established streets which followed the contours of the land or preferences of the homeowners, not an artificial rectangular grid. St. Anne's chapel, built in 1723 in what is today the Roman Catholic cemetery, housed the faith of the residents. Continuing an architectural style originally developed for warmer climates, the French constructed their homes in French Colonial style. Large, expansive porches encircled the homes, ensuring cool breezes throughout. The roofs slanted in a continuous line from gable to eaves. Logs for construction were laid not horizontally flat but vertically upright, originally set directly into the ground (*poteaux en terre*) and later on a log foundation (*poteaux sur sole*). Streets before the houses preserved French family names. For generations, Prairie du Rocher physically resembled a typical French community.

Culturally, the community maintained its French heritage just as strongly. In the church, on the streets, in the schools, and in the homes, the French language predominated for over two centuries. According to contemporary recollections, the dialect of both black and white residents resembled the "more broken" Cajun French rather than modern French. In the homes, French cooks continued Old Country recipes. On New Year's Eve, habitants celebrated "La Gui Année," when revelers in costume roamed door to door, singing in French for an invitation for food and drink. On Saturday nights, farmers brought produce and livestock to town and stayed until midnight, transforming the homes and taverns of small floodplain towns into dancing and socializing centers.

Inevitably, though, the town and group changed. Anglo-Americans and Germans arrived, modifying the town both physically and culturally. A sizable number of German and Anglo-American tombstones in the village's cemetery attest to this demographic shift. For a time, though, these ethnic contacts reinforced rather than diminished group identity. For example, even into the 1930s, according to one Prairie du Rocher resident, one could hear "a good deal" of French, suggesting that "we were better French" back then because "we had to stand up to the Germans."

Not all the changes reinforced the persistence of the French community. The town's primarily Roman Catholic majority declined from an estimated 95 percent to about 60 percent today. Rural school consolidation brought the mostly French-speaking children into contact with "outsiders." More recent national trends in marketing brought corporate-owned stores to the county seat and nearby metropolitan areas, forcing some of the village's mom-and-pop grocery stores and taverns to close. Paved roads and interstate highways provided easy escape routes from the floodplain for shoppers and socializers.

Is "Rocher" (as both residents and nonresidents call it) still French today? One rarely hears French spoken now, and people no longer maintain "their old customs as much as they did years ago," one resident lamented. In contrast, a non-French resident felt that her neighbors "are so Frenchy you can't hardly understand them." While some structures have disappeared, such as the original chapel, others remain; even the new community building has been constructed in French *poteaux en terre* style, preserving the tradition in a new guise. Today, Rocher's street signs and business names, homes and narrow winding streets profess a French identity.

Prairie du Rocher maintains pride in its French heritage, in part drawing strength from perceived contrasts with neighboring groups. As one resident commented; "It was said that after a few drinks the Irish would fight; the Germans would argue; but the French would become friends." Rocher's residents would feel that this camaraderie has allowed them to persist as a group for over two centuries.

Plate 2.1. Site of Village of Kaskaskia
At one time a sizable French and Anglo-American community and the first state capital, the town was located near the confluence of the Kaskaskia and the Mississippi rivers, center of photo. Floods in both 1844 and in 1881 forced the Mississippi into the Kaskaskia's channel, thereby inundating and finally destroying the town.

Plate 2.2. Kaskaskia-Cahokia Trail, Chester Vicinity
The upland, high-water route connected the two French communities through the Illinois prairies. Today segments of the trail lie beneath Illinois Route 3.

Plate 2.3. Prairie du Rocher Vicinity
The road, the old Kaskaskia-Cahokia Trail, skirts the bluffs, thereby preserving the flat, fertile floodplain for farms. Fencerows and utility lines often delimit the narrow boundaries of eighteenth century French *arpents* (land grants) instead of the angular township-range survey lines of the later Anglo-American land surveys.

Plate 2.4. Prairie du Rocher Vicinity

Plate 2.5. Menard House, Ellis Grove Vicinity
Situated at the foot of the bluffs overlooking the site of Kaskaskia, the French Colonial home, built in 1802, reflects the affluence of its former owner, Pierre Menard, a successful merchant and influential politician. This plantation style home features a veranda on piers, which wraps around three sides of the structure.

Plate 2.6. *Menard House, Ellis Grove Vicinity*
The gabled roof of the house is dormered to let in light and for ventilation. The kitchen building in the rear was separate and connected to the main house by an open porch.

Plate 2.7. Creole House, Prairie du Rocher
Started in 1755, a south section was added to the house in 1800 and a northern extension in 1855. The wide *galerie* (porch) and continuous roofline indicate French Colonial architecture.

Plate 2.8. View from Creole House, Prairie du Rocher
The old, low-water Kaskaskia-Cahokia Trail has become the main street through town. Notice the French family name on the small grocery store in the left foreground. The mill in the background marks the modern road to Fort de Chartres.

Plate 2.9. Cletus Pierre Menard Community Building, Prairie du Rocher
Although a contemporary structure, the building reflects the earliest
French construction style, *poteaux en terre*, vertical logs set in trenches.
Compare the wide porch, sloping roofline, and vertical timber construction to the Menard House, Johnson Cabin, Creole House, and the Modoc Cabin.

Plate 2.10. Johnson Cabin, Prairie du Rocher
Built by the Du Frenne family in the early 1800s. Note the French street
sign in the foreground, one of several in Prairie du Rocher preserving
French family names. The cabin is scheduled for demolition.

Plate 2.11. Rear, Johnson Cabin, Prairie du Rocher
A residence until recently, the house had been extensively remodeled both
inside and out, including the enclosure of the back porch and the covering
of logs with clapboards and tar paper.

23

Plate 2.12. Rear Wall Detail, Johnson Cabin, Prairie du Rocher
Vertical timbers placed on the horizontal log sill, in *poteaux sur sole* construction technique, are typical of late eighteenth century French Colonial construction. The foundation consists of dry-laid, unfinished limestone.

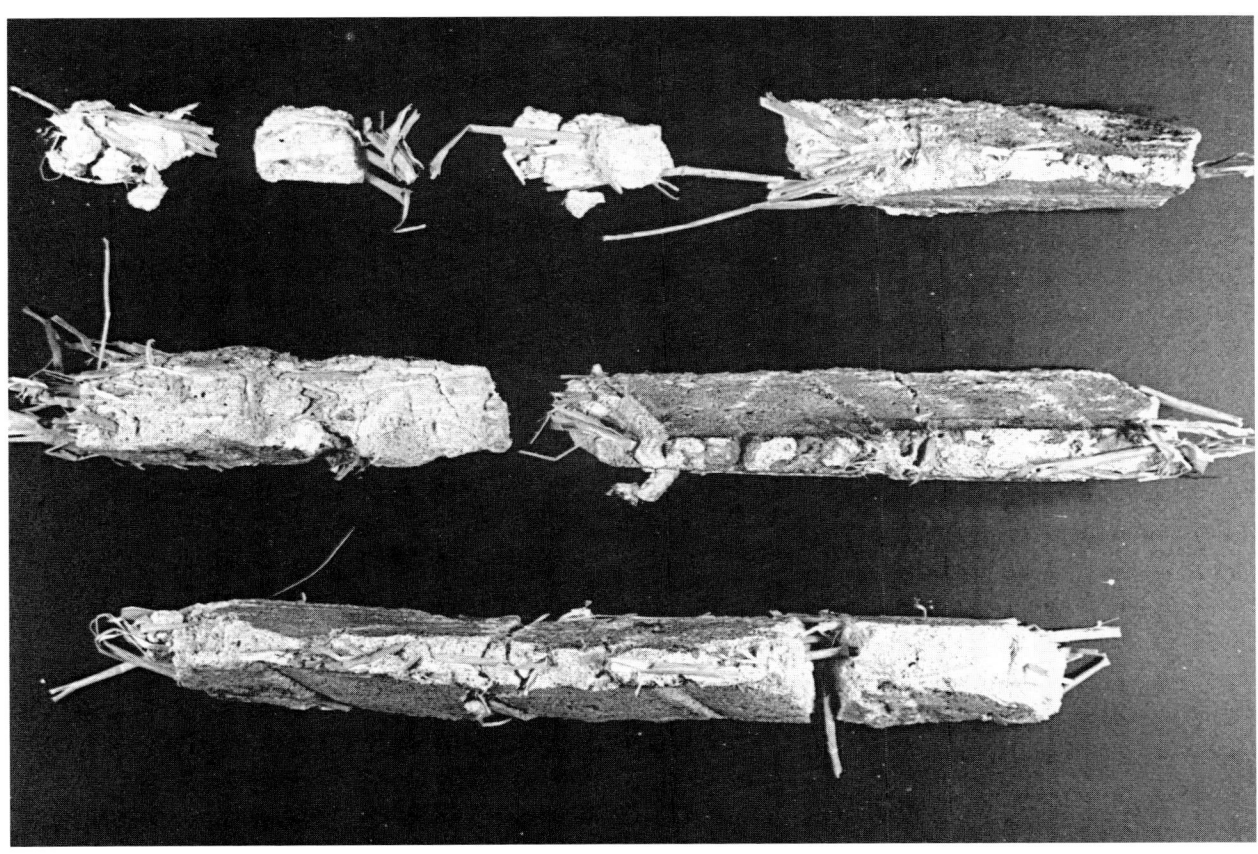

Plate 2.13. Chinking, Johnson Cabin, Prairie du Rocher
Note wheat straw in chinking mixture which also includes a variety of pieces of clothing and hair. In the earliest French structures, a mixture of clay and grass, called *bousillage*, was used to fill spaces between logs.

Plate 2.14. Stone Silo, Prairie du Rocher
Silo, now demolished, constructed c. 1916 of local white limestone, originally on the property of the Conner family.

Plate 2.15. Robert's Store, Prairie du Rocher
This store closed in May 1986 due to competition from larger regional groceries. The stepped gable facade was typical of early twentieth century storefronts, creating the illusion that the building was larger and more substantial than it really was. Owner Everet Robert (now deceased) reminisced, "I used to have an old coal stove in there, and you know how that is. They used to come and sit around that and talk. But those days are not that much anymore. We finally got out of the store."

*Plate 2.16. Tombstone, St. Joseph Cemetery,
    Prairie du Rocher*

A hand-carved sandstone slab, the monument bears the inscription of the stonemason: *Fait par* (made by) J. Belmar. The inscription translates: "Here rests the body of Francis Bachelier, died on 10 April 1871, at the age of 13 months. Missed by his parents."

Plate 2.17. Cabin, Modoc Vicinity
The house sits along the Kaskaskia-Cahokia Trail at the base of the Mississippi bluffs. Now abandoned, the Acadian style house was built of vertical wood boards with soft bricks between them. The walls had been covered with clapboards and tar paper.

Plate 2.18. Detail of North Wall, Cabin, Modoc Vicinity
The brick mortar consists of a sandy clay.

Plate 2.19. Fults House, Fults Vicinity
The log home was constructed in the early nineteenth century by Jacob Fults, whose father had come from Pennsylvania in 1817. The two-story gallery porch spanning the front of the house shows the influence of French architectural traditions in the area.

Plate 2.20. Cabin, Grand Tower Vicinity
This structure has log floor joists but is otherwise frame. The house, approximately seventy-five years old, has a gallery porch formed by the sloping roofline and is typical of vernacular French architecture.

3. The Anglo-Americans

Anglo-American settlers to the region arrived in relatively large numbers after the Revolutionary War. Having served under George Rogers Clark in the western campaigns or having heard about the richness and the availability of land from veterans returning to the eastern states, settlers headed west to Illinois. Many came from the southern states of Virginia, the Carolinas, Kentucky, and Tennessee, down the highways of the Cumberland, Tennessee, and Ohio rivers. Some settlers pushed northward from the southern tip of Illinois into the frontier of the Illinois country, while others remained along the river in order to maintain close access to this important transportation route. Still others sought homesteads and farm fields near already-established French communities such as Prairie du Rocher and Kaskaskia in the Mississippi floodplain.

Culturally, the "Americans" (as the English-speaking pioneers were called) differed greatly from their French neighbors. Scots-Irish Presbyterians and American Baptists and Methodists had little in common with French Roman Catholics. English-speaking customers could not converse with French-speaking merchants in the older towns. The French love of the "good life" angered many temperate Americans. Seeking cheaper land and greater solitude, a multitude of Americans left the floodplains for the hills to modify the Illinois landscape in a new way.

The timbered foothills and hollows above the floodplains and in the southern Ozarks reminded many Americans of their former Appalachian homes. More importantly, the newcomers possessed the technology and skills needed to clear and farm upland environments. Thus many pioneers began pushing up the creeks to the edge of the rolling prairies beyond. This allowed the utilization of several environmental niches simultaneously. Because of real and perceived threats of Native American retaliation, early settlers clustered their homes near permanent water supplies, sheltered within wooden stockades guarded by blockhouses.

For these structures, the Americans utilized log construction materials due to their availability, just like their French neighbors; however, construction techniques contrasted sharply. Over a century earlier, Scandinavian and German settlers in the Atlantic seaboard had passed to the Americans the technique of horizontal log construction, unlike the French vertical method. To connect the timbers, logs were notched and fitted together. While various notching styles may at one time have differentiated regional origins for their makers, by the late eighteenth century styles varied mainly by builder. In general, though, more complicated notching styles marked more permanent structures.

By the early nineteenth century, large migrations of settlers from the Upland South moved into southern Illinois via the Ohio River route. These populations from western Kentucky, central and western Tennessee, and the Carolinas found easy access to the area at Shawneetown, Ford's Ferry in Hardin County, Elizabethtown, Golconda, and

Cairo. These English-speaking settlers became the majority population, and thus no cultural distinctions persisted to demarcate the group.

Despite the concomitant arrival of New England Yankees and their architectural influences, by the first decades of the nineteenth century ethnic patterns had changed. The Anglo-Americans and their cultural characteristics now served as the basis upon which succeeding immigrant waves defined themselves, based on similarities or differences with the majority. The Anglo-American architectural patterns, eventually subject to the fluctuations of general national trends, likewise became the basis upon which to compare later alternatives. Approximately within one generation, the Americans had reshaped both the physical and cultural landscape of southern Illinois by becoming the dominant group.

Because Anglo-Americans formed the majority group and thus shaped the dominant culture, they disappeared from the landscape as an ethnic minority. From the perspective of later groups, who in many cases eventually outnumbered Anglo-Americans in specific regions, it seemed as if the Americans simply vanished. In fact, the Americans persisted by blending completely.

Plate 3.1. Kaskaskia-Cahokia Trail, Waterloo Vicinity
The old trail runs southward from the left foreground through the notch in the horizon between the trees, eventually disappearing beneath Illinois Route 3. Moore Cemetery lies to the right of the notch.

Plate 3.2. Bellefontaine Site, Waterloo Vicinity
Formerly surrounded by a palisade for protection of the pioneers and livestock, the knoll was the site of the Bellefontaine Settlement, also called Moore's Station. To the left-center sets the Moore House and to the right the Moore Cabin. The Kaskaskia-Cahokia Trail runs right-left at the horizon line.

Plate 3.3. Bellefontaine Spring, Waterloo Vicinity
"Beautiful Spring" in French, the water bubbles out behind the Moore House. The spring lies strategically at the edge of the prairie near the crest of a hollow in the Mississippi bluffs along the upland Kaskaskia-Cahokia Trail.

Plate 3.4. James Moore Cabin, Waterloo Vicinity
Moore, a veteran of George Rogers Clark's Illinois campaigns, left the French town of Kaskaskia and founded the Anglo-American settlement at Bellefontaine about 1779. The cabin, of V-notched logs, sits on its original site. Note the encroaching suburbs of Waterloo in the right background.

Plate 3.5. Moore House, Waterloo Vicinity
Although completed as a brick residence in 1872, the core of the building dates approximately to 1780. Preserved within, "all covered over with plaster," is the original log blockhouse for the pioneer settlement of Bellefontaine, according to a local historian. Like most frontier blockhouses, the lower walls served as part of the palisade, while the upper story overarched the lower, a strategy to protect the walls from attack.

Plate 3.6. McRoberts House, Maeystown Vicinity
Born in Scotland in the mid-1700s, McRoberts served under George Rogers Clark and later homesteaded "McRoberts Meadows" southwest of Waterloo. Here he constructed this two-story log house in 1798, today covered with siding. The mantelpiece from this structure was removed and later used by a German settler as a center pier for a barn (see Plate 4.15). The settler's great-grandson, Halbert Mueller stated, "When my great-grandfather bought this place there was a little like a curse over it; nobody wanted to buy it. There was some gold buried with a curse. And there was an eternal light that looked like, I guess, these modern light bulbs. They lived here for years, and that light got dimmer and soon it faded. Now they don't know if whoever was involved dug for that gold or whether the curse wore off."

Plate 3.7. Notching Detail, Log Cabin, Waterloo
This cabin's construction features a combination of V-notching and half-dovetail notching, which may indicate that two different builders worked on the cabin. Half-dovetail notching is considered one of the best notching techniques because the outward slope of notches allows rainwater to drain away, thus decreasing decay. The cabin has been relocated from its original site to rest behind the Peterstown House.

Plate 3.8. William Biggs Cabin, Waterloo
Dating approximately to 1790, the cabin illustrates the V-notching technique. Biggs, a veteran with George Rogers Clark, originally settled at Bellefontaine but later moved to a site several miles north of what is today Waterloo. It was from that farm that the cabin had been removed, and it now rests behind the Peterstown House.

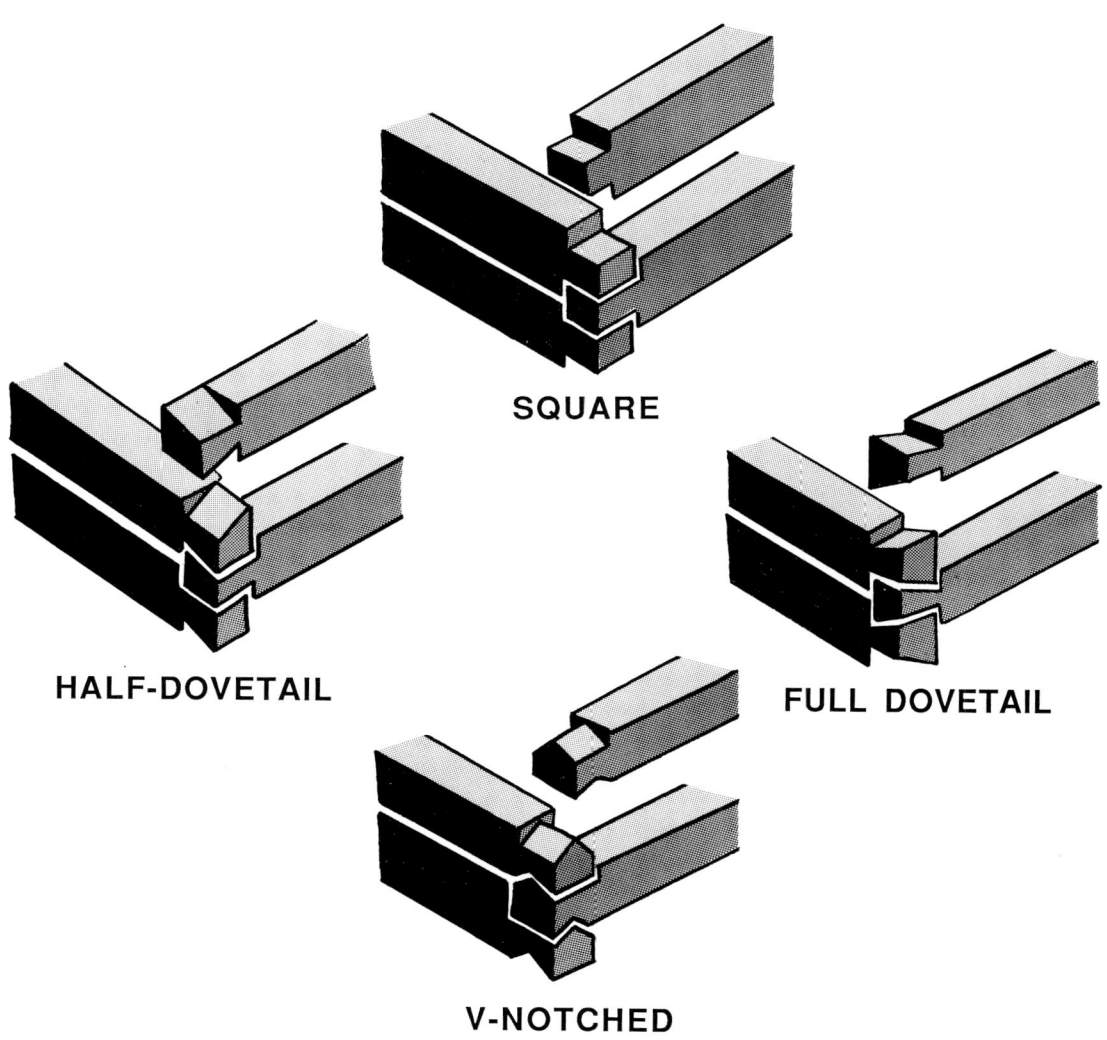

Notching Techniques

Plate 3.9. Peterstown House, Waterloo
Begun about 1816 by Emory Peter Rogers, the hotel and tavern served travelers along the upland Kaskaskia-Cahokia Trail, now Main Street (foreground). Since Rogers' family had come from New England, the house reflects the simple and symmetrical Yankee architectural style. The second floor features a large ballroom. The north part of Waterloo, founded in 1818, originally had been named Peterstown, after Rogers.

Plate 3.10. Panorama, Golconda
View overlooking levee along the Ohio River. Golconda, originally named Sarahville after the wife of one of the first founders, became the seat of Pope County and an important trading center due to its location on the Ohio River. A ferry operated here as early as 1800.

Plate 3.11. Panorama, Golconda
Bluff terrain in background.

Plate 3.12. Panorama, Golconda
View of river from the levee.

Plate 3.13. First Presbyterian Church, Golconda
Built in 1869, the parish was organized in 1819 and is the oldest Presbyterian parish in Illinois. The building exhibits a blending of Greek temple form, which is expressed in exterior walls divided by vertical recessed panels, and Romanesque influences such as arched windows and doorways.

Plate 3.14. Richard Taylor House, Golconda
Common I-house construction characterized by its one-room depth, two full stories, and entrance in the long side of the structure. Additions on the back of such houses are usually later renovations. Photo by Guy G. Weaver.

Plate 3.15. Downtown View, Elizabethtown
Elizabethtown was an established community as early as 1812 and an important steamboat stop for trade and passengers. It is now the seat of Hardin County. In typical Upland South fashion, the county courthouse was built on a prominence in the center of a regular grid pattern of streets and lanes. Photo by Guy G. Weaver.

Plate 3.16. Rose Hotel, Elizabethtown
The original west section of the hotel was built in 1814 by James McFarland, founder of Elizabethtown. Major additions to the structure were made in subsequent years. The two-story porch, facing the river, is indicative of French vernacular architecture in the Midwest. Photo by Guy G. Weaver.

Plate 3.17. Lightner House, Elizabethtown
Early 1800s structure constructed of locally produced brick. It is built in the typical I-house form but of solid brick construction with no framing; the first floor walls are fourteen inches thick. The original owner named the house "Glen Echo."

Plate 3.18. Davis Log Cabin, Herod
This cabin was built c. 1926 and served as a roadhouse.

Plate 3.19. Cabin, Eichorn Vicinity
The logs in this cabin are barely notched and secured with wire nails. Photo by Guy G. Weaver.

Plate 3.20. St. Patrick's Roman Catholic Church, Cairo
Historical photo of the parish founded in 1838 to serve the Irish Catholic laborers brought in to construct a state-proposed railroad from Cairo to La Salle. The present Romanesque style building was erected in 1894.

Plate 3.21. Front Entryway, St. Patrick's Roman Catholic Church, Cairo
The exterior stonework and elaborate classical treatment of the rounded arched doorway surmounted by a pediment and the double doors flanked by a set of columns are indicative of Romanesque styling.

Plate 3.22. Landscape, Cobden Vicinity
Originally known as South Pass, the town was incorporated as Cobden in 1859. Settlers before 1850 generally came from the Upland South. After the building of the Illinois Central Railroad, many New Englanders were attracted to the area's orchard lands.

Plate 3.23 Bailey House, Jonesboro
Built c. 1855 by local contractor Nelson Lingle, this house is believed to be the oldest in Jonesboro. The exterior walls are constructed of brick and are eighteen inches thick. The foundation of the house, rear steps, sidewalk leading to the street, and retaining walls are all constructed of native limestone.

Plate 3.24. Coomes House, Jonesboro
This brick L-shaped house is believed to have been built in 1856. The main part of the house is flanked by chimneys at each gable.

Plate 3.25. St. Ann's Episcopal Church, Anna
The cornerstone of the church was laid in 1886. The fieldstone structure is built in Gothic Revival style, characterized by the overall vertical emphasis of the building, its steep gabled roof, and lancet-shaped windows.

Plate 3.26. Double Pen House, Macedonia
A double pen house is characteristically made up of two rooms covered by a common roof. Each room usually possesses an outside door with a chimney present on one or both gable ends of the house. Photo by Guy G. Weaver.

Plate 3.27. Log Barn, Piopolis
This barn is probably very old, as evidenced by the use of massive timbers in the construction of the frame. Early settlers had access to the abundance of mature trees available in the virgin forests for use as large beams and structural supports.

Plate 3.28. Notching Detail, Log Cabin, Piopolis
The corner joining on this single pen (one-room) log cabin shows the use of square notching. Although easier to use, square notching is also less structurally stable, attesting to the fact that many Anglo-American settlers regarded log houses as only temporary structures.

Plate 3.29. Pegging Detail, Log Cabin, Piopolis
The use of pegging to secure logs can be seen in this detail of a doorframe.

4. The Germans

German immigrants entered southern Illinois in large numbers beginning in the 1830s and continuing for the next fifty years or so. During this time, Germany actually consisted of a variety of loosely confederated or independent kingdoms, provinces, duchies, and autonomous cities; the newcomers from that diversity displayed the same heterogeneity of accents, customs, and even motivations for leaving. Many desired the political freedom and economic opportunity in the United States, especially when compared with that of Europe. Illinois, legally a nonslave and apparently a prosperous state, possessed a moral and an economic attraction that many other states lacked. Equally compelling were the emotional tugs of friends and relatives who had already settled here. German immigrants, because they came in such large numbers to southwestern Illinois at a relatively early time, had a substantial cultural and physical impact on the land, one that persists today.

The majority of German immigrants came to the area from two general regions: the northwest and southwest of present-day West Germany. While most other variations in custom and accent from the Old Country faded relatively rapidly, the geographical and cultural distinctions between the northern (Low) Germans and the southern (High) Germans persisted, even influencing the settlement patterns in the area. The High Germans, from the more upland regions, preferred hillier terrain for their primarily grain farms. Thus they tended to select sites like Maeystown and Waterloo, located respectively in the hilly terraces of the bluffs or rolling prairies just above. Even in more southerly and isolated High German communities such as Piopolis, grain farming was pursued and a rural lifestyle established. In contrast, Germantown's founders emigrated largely from the kingdom of Hanover and nearby regions further north in Europe, thus flatter and traditionally more conducive to dairy farming. Cultural and linguistic differences demarcated these two groups well into the twentieth century.

Physically, the landscape changed under the direction of these new arrivals. They founded or expanded towns, often naming them after cities in their homeland. Street names, too, preserved Old Country place names: Westfal, Munster, and Hanover streets in Germantown, for example, recall the names of the German-speaking regions of Westphalia, Münster, and Hanover. Many German immigrants were skilled masons or carpenters, and thus they crafted well-built homes, churches, and commercial sites, providing southwestern Illinois with a distinctly German-American architectural style. Breweries, another German technological and cultural contribution, supplied neighborhood taverns proliferating along tidy streets. To maintain the liveliness and gemütlichkeit of the Old Country, Germans fashioned their new environment to resemble as much as possible the one they remembered leaving behind.

Communities, particularly the smaller ones like Germantown, Maeystown, and Piopolis, remained German well into the twentieth century. Customs such as holiday festivities for *Fastnacht* (the night before the Lenten fast begins) or St. Nicholas Day

(December 6, when children received small gifts) helped distinguish Germans from their non-German neighbors. Congregations in these communities used the German language in church services into the 1930s, well after the anti-German xenophobia of World War I. Older residents spoke German in businesses and homes. Communities remained closely knit and valued familial events such as confirmations and weddings as significant social occasions.

Today, both physically and culturally, the landscape of southern Illinois contains "German" communities, as both Germans and non-Germans recognize. While "a lot of the little houses are gone," as one resident lamented, numerous examples nevertheless line the streets, professing the brickmason's and stonemasons' art. Even today, "almost everyone has a garden," a younger resident of Germantown noted. Taverns, still important socializing centers, dot many street corners. The German language, whether *Plattdeutsch* or *Hochdeutsch*, may still be heard occasionally, but today older residents primarily speak it for recreation. Nonetheless, a noticeably characteristic accent persists; an accent by which words become "upside down or backwards." "I don't care how long they've gone to school or anything else, it's just there, and it comes out," as one woman put it. This accent conspicuously distinguishes Germans from non-Germans today.

Time and again, German residents have described themselves as stubborn and set in their ways. At the same time, they characterize themselves as frugal, hardworking, and family-oriented. One said, "I believe that Germans are a lot cleaner. You never found your homes run down, ever. Anything gets wrong, it's fixed right now." It may be that these same attributes have enabled the Germans as a group to persist. A local, German-American politician described his job, "I try to keep the town as it's been for the last 150 years." Culturally and physically, this generally describes all German-American communities and their residents in the area today.

Plate 4.1. Hanover Street, Maeystown
St. John's United Church of Christ in the background, built in 1866, crowns a hill above the steeply sloping streets of the village settled in the early 1850s. Note the houses built directly on the street. The site appealed to German immigrants because it resembled the hills of southern Germany. Note, too, the limestone masonry of the town's structures.

Plate 4.2. Bundy Farm, Maeystown
Jacob Maeys, a German immigrant, purchased "McRoberts Meadows" in 1848 and laid out a town later named for him. The low white building with the stone foundation is Maeys' original cabin, built as a double pen and relocated downslope from the right about twenty yards. Maeys' more permanent house, built about the time of the Civil War, stands to the right.

Plate 4.3. Springhouse, Waterloo Vicinity
The homesteader immigrated to southwestern Illinois from Germany in the 1840s and built several outbuildings for his farm, including the springhouse, by the 1860s.

Plate 4.4. Springhouse Interior, Waterloo Vicinity
The handmade wooden buckets still draw cool water from the depths of the well. Note the wooden shelf in the foreground, worn from use, and the carpentry work.

Plate 4.5. Outdoor Bake Oven, Waterloo Vicinity
Built before 1860, the oven was constructed of limestone and brick with an iron door. "Good German" bread was baked here until the roof collapsed sometime in the 1970s. Note the wooden table to the right and the bread paddle to the left, still in place.

Plate 4.6. Platz House, Columbia Vicinity
Built in 1850, this stone structure features Greek Revival styling, popular with Germans in this area. The one-and-a-half-story house has a long, sloping roof terminating over wide porches. Originally a French introduction, these spacious porches became standard on farms throughout midwestern prairies. A carved cornerstone set high in the right side wall bears Platz's name and the date of construction.

Plate 4.7. Cellar, Werling House, Waterloo Vicinity
This view shows a detail of the stone masonry *Archkeller*, or cellar, used for storing apples, potatoes, preserved foods, beer, and wine. Built in the 1840s, the house was said at one time to have been a post on the Underground Railroad for a tunnel supposedly extends from beneath the house under a road to a nearby field.

Plate 4.8. Front Door, Buss House, Waterloo Vicinity
Buss, a local miller, built the house of native sandstone in 1858. The sandstone door and window frames are intricately carved and bear an inscription above the door. The house sits just north of the Brinkmann House on a knoll above a creek.

Plate 4.9. Detail of Sandstone Lintel, Buss House, Waterloo Vicinity
The hand-carved German inscription translates: "God with us. Built by B. Heinrich Buss and M. Theresia Buss in the year 1858."

Plate 4.10. Gundlach-Grosse House, Columbia
Built c. 1858 by John Gundlach for A. Grosse who held interest in the Monroe Brewery in Columbia. The former owner stored surplus beer in a brick vault beneath the house. The Greek Revival style is typical of homes in this area. Note the ornate cornice and the treatment of the recessed doorway as a classical portico. Window lintels are cast iron.

Plate 4.11. Structural Detail, Hartmann Barn, Waterloo Vicinity
Built by Christian Hartmann in 1872 with local labor. The timbers are white pine with oak pegs. According to the current owner, at one time the barn contained a *Hexelkammer*, a horse-powered mill to separate oats from chaff. Hartmann emigrated from the Grand Duchy of Hesse-Darmstadt in 1852 and purchased the farm in 1865; it is still owned by his descendants.

Plate 4.12. Summer Kitchen, "Stonewood," Columbia Vicinity
The limestone outbuilding served as a summer kitchen. During hot summer months, cooking and other activities were typically conducted in such buildings. This structure has now been demolished.

Plate 4.13. Barn Door, "Stonewood," Columbia Vicinity
Dutch door construction in limestone and timber barn. The door illustrates the stonemasonry and carpentry skills and attention to detail of early local craftsmen. The barn has now been demolished.

Plate 4.14. Barn Window, "Stonewood," Columbia Vicinity

Plate 4.15. Mueller Barn, Maeystown Vicinity
Detail of the stone mantelpiece originally in the nearby McRoberts House (see plate 3.6), now incorporated into the barn's foundation as a center pier. The inscription reads; "JAMES McROBERTS and MARY, his Wife Settled this place in the year of our Lord 1798."

Plate 4.16. Mueller Barn, Maeystown Vicinity
Location of the McRoberts mantelpiece beneath the large logs of the German-built barn. Note the square-notching technique more typical of outbuildings.

*Plate 4.17. Salem-Baum Evangelical Church,
      Maeystown Vicinity*
German-speaking Protestant settlers organized the church in an area southwest of Waterloo in 1845. An original log church was replaced in 1883 by this limestone structure. The congregation disbanded in 1938 and the building burned in the 1970s.

Plate 4.18. Steeple, St. Paul's United Church of Christ, Waterloo

Note the rooster on top, a German tradition representing the bird which crowed three times at Peter's denial of Christ. The three-dimensional copper ornament, whose twin once adorned the Salem-Baum Evangelical Church, was made in Waterloo in 1883.

Plate 4.19. Brinkmann House, Waterloo Vicinity
Oldest part of the house was constructed of timber in 1885. The owners completed the house with local sandstone in 1894. Underneath the house is believed to be a channel, cut into the sandstone bedrock, where a former owner stored *Handkäse* (hand cheese), a foul smelling but popular food.

Plate 4.20. Deerhaake House, Germantown Vicinity
A farmhouse about "one hundred twenty-five or so years old," according to the owner. This home has double entryways characteristic of both frame and brick German homes in the area.

Plate 4.21. St. Boniface Roman Catholic Church, Germantown

The Low German Catholic settlers of the area established the first church in 1839. The present church was dedicated in 1856 and is constructed of stone which was hauled eight miles from Shoal Creek. The walls are over twenty inches thick, and the hardwood floors are original.

Plate 4.22 Interior of Belltower, St. Boniface Roman Catholic Church, Germantown

Note the massive timber construction and the use of pegging to join the structural members. Also note that the wooden pegs have not been cut and smoothed over and that some logs still have bark on them, unfinished perhaps because the work was not intended to be viewed by the public.

Plate 4.23. Tombstone, St. Boniface Roman Catholic Cemetery, Germantown

The inscription exemplifies the birthplace of many of Germantown's early residents: Lotten, in the province of Hanover, northeastern Germany.

Plate 4.24. Station of the Cross, St. Boniface Roman Catholic Cemetery, Germantown

These small shrines, located along a right angle of cemetery roads, provide places for contemplating events in Jesus' crucifixion. Station twelve reads; "Jesus dies on the cross." The plaster figures appear to be hand-painted and are enclosed behind protective glass.

Plate 4.25. Linnemann House, Germantown
Over one hundred years old, this house typifies the many Greek Revival style houses built close to the street in German communities. Note the symmetry of the doors, windows, and even the shrubbery in front.

Plate 4.26. Bartelso Vicinity
In this view, approximately southeast, the relatively flat prairie is punctuated by long, low hills of glacial debris. Low German immigrants began to settle the area in the 1830s, selecting the region partly because it resembled their homeland. The population, however, was rural and widely dispersed, and Bartelso was not incorporated until 1898.

Plate 4.27. Interior, St. Cecilia's Roman Catholic Church, Bartelso

To accommodate the large German population of the area, the church was constructed in 1884. The interior plasterwork of the building was completed in the fall. To prevent the plaster from freezing, stoves were installed in the church, and fires were maintained during construction.

Plate 4.28. Jantzen's Store, Bartelso
Vacant for the past ten years or so, the store sits across the street from St. Cecilia's Church. The Jantzens, who arrived first in St. Louis, heard about the newly organized church and thought the community might need a store. Opened in 1885, and selling everything "from soup to nuts," Jantzen's held the town's post office and a popular tavern. Merchants had to speak three languages to serve customers: Low German, High German, and English.

Plate 4.29. Paul Wellen House, Piopolis
The two front rooms were built in 1895 by John Wellen, grandfather of Paul Wellen. An addition was later built on the back. Note the similarity in construction of this and the Herzing House (plate 4.31) which also features two front-facing gables and a double entryway on the first floor.

Plate 4.30. George Stich House, Piopolis
Built in 1898 by Capistron Aydt, who constructed many of the turn-of-the-century homes in Piopolis. The Aydts were among the first German families to settle the Hamilton County community c. 1841. Note the embellishment to the basic I-house form of the facing-gable and bay windows on either side of the first floor entryway. Reverend August Reyling, Pastor, St. John the Baptist Roman Catholic Church, Piopolis, said in 1888, "Many plans were laid to drive out the German Catholics, but they were a stubborn lot and bravely held their own. Luckily the 'Yankees' were foiled in all their plots. The German settlers would not let themselves be scared away but remained, and they remain to the present day."

Plate 4.31. Herzing House, Piopolis
Built in 1918 by local carpenter Capistron Aydt for George and Elizabeth Herzing. The couple had left the Low German Catholic area of Clinton County to settle in Piopolis, a thriving High German Catholic community whose inhabitants had originally come from several villages in the Baden area of southwestern Germany.

Plate 4.32. Rubenacher Barn, Piopolis
This barn, at least eighty-five years old, was reportedly built by Jack Kornet and his family. The barn illustrates a type common among the Pennsylvania Germans and Dutch that subsequently became a standard barn type across rural America.

Plate 4.33. Humm-Pairsh House, Elizabethtown
Built in 1907 by German immigrant Frank Humm and family. Oak cut from the property was used to frame the house. The interior has three-quarter-inch, tongue-and-groove walls. The original roof was constructed of split-wood shingles.

Plate 4.34. Gable Detail, Cano House, Grand Tower
Believed to be the oldest house in the Red Town area of Grand Tower. The embellishment of the facing gables combines Stick Style and Queen Anne influences.

5. The Poles

While a few Polish-speaking railroad workers and their families had settled in a wooded area near DuBois before the Civil War, the vast majority of Polish immigrants arrived several decades later. The flat prairies had been colonized by Anglo-Americans and later by Germans from Protestant and Roman Catholic communities to the west. However, much land remained vacant. As the Illinois Central Railroad pushed through, the company needed workers and, more importantly, residents to ship and to receive goods along the rails. In 1872 John B. Turchin, a Russian-born American Civil War general, opened a land development company, promoting in Poland and in Polish-American communities the inexpensive land in southern Illinois, particularly around what is today Radom. Conflicts arose as Turchin quarreled with competitors, and thus the towns of DuBois and Tamaroa, each several miles further south, grew and became established communities. As the area prospered, it attracted additional Polish immigrants fleeing military and religious persecution. Coal mines and rich agricultural land drew more settlers while simultaneously enhancing the economic vitality of the towns. National immigrant associations provided financial assistance and emotional support to many newcomers. By 1878 several neighboring Polish communities flourished on the prairies.

Culturally, the more recent arrivals caused a drastic shift on the ethnic landscape. The relatively few "Yankees" or "Americans" in the area preferred to remain separate, while the more numerous Germans tended to intermingle and intermarry. Perhaps aiding this assimilation was language. In the 1870s the country which is today Poland was torn between Tsarist Russia and German-speaking Prussia; consequently, many Polish immigrants had learned German in school. Language differences persisted in southern Illinois, of course, but merchants, fluent in Polish, German, and English, thrived. Polish speakers eventually outnumbered the Germans, though, and the lingua franca of Sunday Roman Catholic services became Polish, to the dismay of German residents. Polish predominated in street conversations before World War II. Polish foods, holiday customs, and even dancing styles further delimited groups well into the twentieth century.

Physically, the Poles had less of an impact, perhaps for several reasons. First, many of the immigrants had already lived in the United States, having come from urban areas like Chicago or St. Louis or smaller mining towns in the eastern coalfields. Secondly, because of the easy access to the railroad, sawmill lumber and more professional construction materials could easily be shipped in, tempering vernacular styles. And finally, by the post–Civil War era, national architectural styles had begun to replace regional and folk variations. Generally, Poles did not want to express their identity outwardly by means of unique construction styles; rather, they wanted to build homes like everyone else.

Nevertheless, the Polish newcomers modified their physical landscape. They transformed Old Country place names like Radomsko and Poznán to Radom and Posen. To express their faith, they built Roman Catholic churches in each community and decorated the largest with windows depicting episodes in Polish history or with images of popular Polish saints. Houses, initially of log, were replaced by frame structures, often with a garden and a statue of the Virgin Mary in the yard. In life Polish names proclaimed Polish businesses and in death still enunciated one's heritage, carved forever onto tombstones.

While many of these physical reminders of a Polish heritage remain today, other cultural ties have been modified due to fear or assimilation. "There was a period of time when people felt afraid if they spoke Polish. They wanted to be English and just speak the English language," one resident recalled. To downplay a separate identity, some families Anglicized their names: Mydlarz became Mydler, and Szramkowski became Sherman.

Nevertheless, many Polish cultural characteristics remain vibrant. Most older residents still speak Polish, and a few prefer it to English, their second language. Many younger inhabitants can at least understand Polish as well. Locals recognize a sizable Polish Catholic majority for area communities. A parish priest estimated that about 60 percent of his parishioners confessed in Polish.

Despite the modern highways whisking shoppers and their money to distant places and despite the closing of the mines and decline of the railroads, the residents of the small villages of Tamaroa, Posen, DuBois, Radom, and Scheller still maintain their ethnic identity. Defining characteristics have changed, but the Polish-Americans persist. As one lifelong resident of Radom expressed proudly and vigorously; "We are still mostly Polish around here."

Plate 5.1. Main Street, DuBois
Postcard view from the Illinois Central tracks down Main Street of this "booming" railroad town. On the right in the forefront are Reminger's Store for men's clothing and the town hall. On the left in the forefront are a saloon, the undertaker's, and harness maker's establishments. About this time, residents recalled, the town contained about a thousand people "and four or five saloons." Historical photo taken c. 1908 courtesy of Eugene Waldman, DuBois.

Plate 5.2. Nikrant Barn, DuBois Vicinity
Cabin of the Gondek family, one of the area's earliest Polish pioneers, who had left Indiana in the 1860s to work on the Illinois Central Railroad. The logs for this cabin had been cut by hand, including the row of chiseled-out notches for rafters supporting an upper story. The exterior had at one time been covered with clapboards, while the interior walls had been covered with wooden lathes and then plastered.

Plate 5.3. Nikrant Barn, DuBois Vicinity
Today used as a storage shed, the barn originally was built as a log home. Note the corner notching detail and the chinking that still remains between the logs.

Plate 5.4. Kuhn Hardware Store, DuBois
Built in the mid-nineteenth century by Adam Kuhn, a prominent German entrepreneur who was already well established in the area by the time of the Poles' arrival. Kuhn owned coal mines, a hardware store, and more than half of the land in the area—and served as president of the bank. Historical photo courtesy of Eugene Waldman, DuBois.

Plate 5.5. Kuhn House, DuBois
Now abandoned, the home adjoined the Kuhn Store directly across the street from the town hall. The location is not coincidental, for at one time the Kuhn family "owned the town," several residents recalled. The town even bore the unofficial name "Kuhnville" for a while. Note the ornate iron fence and expansive yard of the house, indirect evidence of the former owners' prosperity. Even the sidewalk is wider in front of the home than it is on other streets.

Plate 5.6. St. Charles Borromeo Roman Catholic Church, DuBois
Front of the church during construction. The church was planned by Father (later Monsignor) Joseph Ceranski, who served the parish for sixty-four years. Historical photo, taken c. 1908, courtesy of Eugene Waldman, DuBois.

Plate 5.7. St. Charles Borromeo Roman Catholic Church, DuBois
The statue above the door is that of the church's Italian namesake; the inscription is in Polish. Twin towers reach a peak of 116 feet, and the front of the church extends 80 feet in width. Originally established in 1868, the parish outgrew its first church (built in 1877), and construction for the new church began in 1908.

Plate 5.8. Holy Scapular Society, DuBois
A DuBois women's religious organization founded in 1879, the group stands before St. Charles Borromeo Roman Catholic Church. Assimilation may be inferred by comparing the dress of the woman (a Polish immigrant) on the far right, front row, with that of her daughter, second from the left, front row. Historical photo, taken c. 1929, courtesy of Mary Ksycki, DuBois.

Plate 5.9. St. Mark's United Church of Christ and St. Charles Borromeo Roman Catholic Church (background), DuBois

St. Charles Borromeo Church was nicknamed the Cathedral of the Prairies. The size of the two churches provides an estimate of the number of German Protestant and Polish Roman Catholic groups in the area.

Plate 5.10. Ksycki Store, DuBois
The store opened in 1911. Benches in front of the store provided a "nice meeting place" for men to sit and chat. Helping his trade, Mr. Ksycki spoke German, English, and Polish to his customers. Historical photo courtesy of Mary Ksycki, DuBois.

Plate 5.11. Ksycki Store, DuBois
Privately owned painting of the building, which has been destroyed. In the original store, built on land purchased from the Illinois Central Railroad, the double door on the left led to the section where hardware and dry goods were sold. On the right-hand side, the grocery sold fruits, vegetables, canned goods, and preserved meats. "It was more like a trading place," Mary Ksycki recalled. "The storekeepers didn't have money; people couldn't bring in their produce and expect cash. It was a matter of bringing in their eggs, chickens, ducks, whatever they had, and then buying things that would more or less equal what they had brought in."

Plate 5.12 Chapel Hill School, DuBois Vicinity
The building typifies the ubiquitous one-room schoolhouses that dotted southern Illinois. Here pupils learned the basics and learned them well, a former school teacher recalled. Most of her students spoke Polish, even though they weren't allowed to speak it in school. Historical photo, taken c. 1929, courtesy of Mary Ksycki, DuBois.

Plate 5.13. Main Thoroughfare, Radom
The town began about 1873, due primarily to John Turchin's promotions for various land companies. Radom grew slowly, overshadowed by DuBois four miles south yet anchored by the railroad and area coal mines. As both gradually declined in economic importance, the town's population stabilized. In the background towers the steeple of St. Michael's Roman Catholic Church, constructed in 1923 to replace an 1873 wooden building.

Plate 5.14. Szopinski Store, Radom
The store, over one hundred years old, is located near the Illinois Central tracks and still does a lively business. Note the bay window on the second floor of the building and the stepped additions, which appear to be later renovations. According to local residents, Radom contains about 90 percent Polish Roman Catholics.

Plate 5.15. Crucifixion Shrine, St. Michael's Roman Catholic Cemetery, Radom Vicinity
According to a locally interpreted Old World custom, men were interred in one row, women in another, and children in a third. Just beyond the covered altar lies the oldest part of the cemetery, where the custom seems to have been followed. Husbands were not buried next to wives but were placed in a separate row to the left of the shrine, and children younger than fourteen were inhumed in a single row to the right. The practice appears to have died out in the early twentieth century.

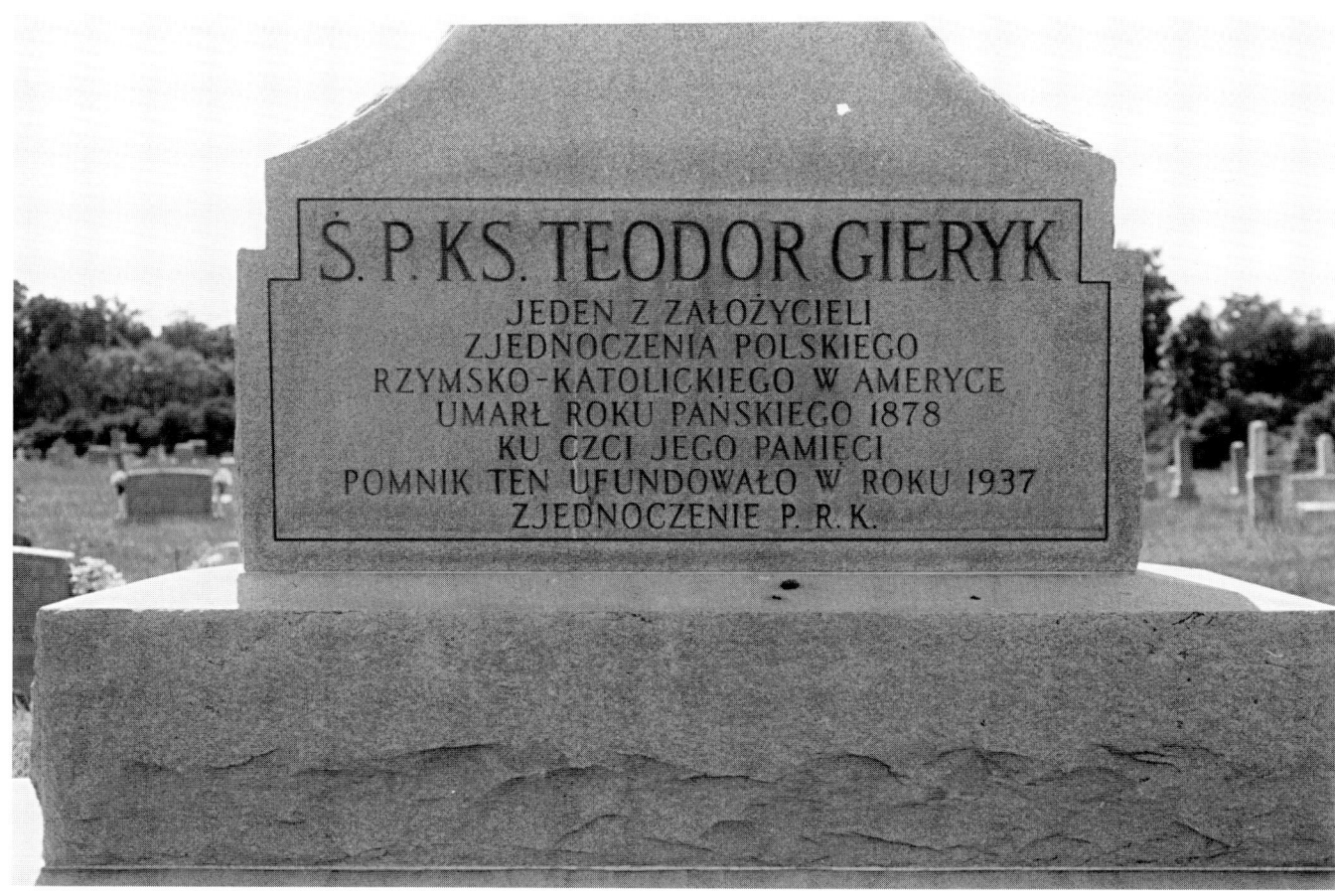

Plate 5.16. Monument, St. Michael's Roman Catholic Cemetery, Radom Vicinity
The inscription reads: "Rest in peace Father Teodor Gieryk, one of the founders of the Polish Roman Catholic Organization in America. He died in the year of Our Lord 1878. In the honor of his memory, this monument was erected in the year 1937. The Polish Roman Catholic Organization." Such organizations provided financial assistance and settlement advice for immigrants. Father Gieryk, the first pastor at St. Michael's, has been reinterred in Chicago.

Plate 5.17. Station of the Cross, St. Michael's Roman Catholic Church, Radom

Lining the interior walls of the church, the stations depict events in Jesus' crucifixion. The inscription for station twelve reads: "Jesus on the cross dies."

Plate 5.18 Main Thoroughfare, Posen
Not located on the Illinois Central main line and thus not a targeted Polish colony, Posen was settled primarily by Polish immigrant farmers around 1875. Not even a crossroads today, Posen mainly consists of this street with a business and residential district extending along both sides of a rural road for about two city blocks.

6. The Italians

Attracted to southern Illinois for several reasons, Italian immigrants arrived in large numbers during the last few decades of the nineteenth century. Many fled oppressive poverty in Italy; others sought economic opportunity here. The principal magnet was coal. As the mines opened, owners needed workers, and thousands of Italian-speaking newcomers populated the coal-mining towns of the region. While numerous families came from Italian neighborhoods in St. Louis and other American communities, most came directly from Italy, bringing their cultural and linguistic regional distinctions along with their clothes and dreams. Devoutly Roman Catholic, most were northern Italians from the Piedmont and Lombardy regions, including the little town of Cuggione near Milan. While they settled in numerous and prosperous coal-mining towns throughout southern Illinois, the Italians centered their attention on Herrin. To this day, Herrin still bears the cultural and physical imprint of this group.

Herrin had been established since 1816; thus, the Italians had little opportunity to restructure the city completely. In fact, according to some residents, the Anglo-American majority preferred it that way. The Italians occasionally faced antagonism from the Americans in the early twentieth century, ranging from schoolyard epithets to adult ostracism. Unlike the German or French communities, no streets in Herrin bear Old Country names; a sign, one resident felt, of the resentment perceived by the immigrants. Despite this real and perceived antagonism, the Italians physically modified Herrin.

The Illinois Central Railroad tracks bisect Herrin, and the newcomers selected homes primarily on the north side. At first, neighborhoods preserved Old Country regional loyalties, as southern Italians, Lombards, and Piedmontese remained in separate clusters. Initially, individuals from different regions rarely socialized because "they talked different," according to a member of one group. These social and linguistic distinctions gradually faded as assimilation commenced; however, residents maintained a knowledge of their ancestral homeland for generations. The northwest business district became a "Little Italy," bustling with shops, stores, and taverns catering to immigrant families. Whether due to social ostracism or self-described "clannishness," Italians formed mutual-aid associations or clubs. The Rome Club and the C. C. (Christopher Columbus) Club provided men with financial loans and yearly dividends as well as taverns for socializing. At the Lombard Society Store, cash-poor Italian residents could purchase meat, dry goods, and groceries on credit or borrow money for home construction. Italians transformed their neighborhoods by planting vegetable gardens and building grape arbors. To continue Old World culture, they constructed an opera house, said to have been modeled after Milan's. To profess their faith, they built Our Lady of Mt. Carmel Roman Catholic Church in an Italianate architectural style. In San Carlo Cemetery, Italian tombstones, often bearing small photographs of the deceased, preserved the native language of the newcomers.

Culturally, the Italians maintained an ethnic unity, largely in spite of Old Country regional variations in dialect. In the stores and clubs, immigrants spoke Italian, passing much of the language on to the next generation. On Sunday afternoons, old men used that language to enliven *boccie* (lawn bowling) games. Several Italian bakeries produced breads and other delicacies. Herrin's butcher shops sold locally made salami; the grocery stores stocked imported and local ingredients for Italian dishes. Cures from the Old Country continued to heal the sick, and midwives delivered babies using traditional techniques. In many ways, the rich and vibrant cultural traditions of Italy took root and thrived in Herrin.

Today, those streets still reflect that Italian heritage but in a less direct way. The opera house burned in 1917; the Lombard Store closed and burned; and the C. C. and Rome Club buildings have been sold. One *boccie* court has become a parking lot. Few people publicly speak Italian, but it can be heard occasionally. The Roman Catholic church endures as the focal point of a thriving and devout congregation. The forty-six remaining members of the Christopher Columbus Cooperative Association continue to receive annual dividends. The Town Bakery, using the traditional recipe, produces Italian bread, and a few stores still sell locally made Italian foods. Grape arbors and gardens ornament many of the neat yards of houses in former Italian neighborhoods. Families perpetuate traditional Italian recipes, and a few residents have taught folk songs to their grandchildren. In Herrin and surrounding towns, an Italian group persists.

Analogous to a stone dropped in a pond, the impact of Herrin's Italian immigrants might best be described as a series of ripples, subtly but deeply transforming the physical and cultural surface of the community.

Plate 6.1. Northeast Commercial District, Herrin
As a part of "Little Italy," the neighborhood once bustled with Italian social life. Just up the street to the right stood the Lombard Society Store, a combination grocery store, meat market, and dry goods store that closed during the Depression. In the center of the photo is the C. C. Club. One block to the north is the Rome Club.

Plate 6.2. Rome Club, Herrin
One of the essential Italian mutual-aid organizations in Herrin. Classical forms used to embellish the building are apparent in the brickwork frieze and entryway. About ten years ago, the club disbanded and the building was sold to the Elks Club.

Plate 6.3. Rome Club, Herrin
Detail of the ornate, friezelike brickwork in the center of the building above second-story windows. While the hall was not built until 1909, Italians organized the club itself in 1901 as a mutual-aid society as well as a social organization.

Plate 6.4. Main Entrance, Rome Club, Herrin
Note the Romanesque-influenced arched entrance, with massive columns.

Plate 6.5. Our Lady of Mt. Carmel Roman Catholic Church, Herrin
Built in the late nineteenth century, the interior of the church was remodeled in the 1950s and much of the original decoration obscured. Note the Italianate style bell tower, the (red) tile roof, and the classical treatment of the main doorway.

Plate 6.6. Our Lady of Mt. Carmel Roman Catholic Church, Herrin
To the right of the church lies a small garden, adjacent to the pastor's residence. Inside the church, many windows bear the names of their Italian donors. One, however,—a green and white depiction of St. Patrick—is inscribed "from the Irish parishioners."

Plate 6.7. Tombstone, San Carlo Roman Catholic Cemetery, Herrin
The inscription translates: "In fondest memory of Pietro Gaudina, veteran of the Italian-Turkish Campaign [1912] and the Great War [World War I]. He died 1 November 1927, aged 37 years, far from his beloved homeland and dearly missed by his adoring family, who are quite inconsolable. A prayer." Photo by John M. Coggeshall.

Plate 6.8. C. C. Club Bar, Herrin
Recently remodeled, the bar has been enclosed with paneling, several booths have been replaced with tables, and a pinball machine and jukebox have been added. The Christopher Columbus Cooperative Association still holds title to the building, although they relinquished informal possession in the early 1980s. To enroll originally, "you had to be from the northern part of Italy."

Plate 6.9. Ballroom Interior Detail, C. C. Club, Herrin
This ship, perhaps representing Christopher Columbus' flagship, adorns the bar in the second-floor ballroom. The bar extends the width of the room.

Plate 6.10. Detail of Stairs to Ballroom, C. C. Club, Herrin
Note the pressed tin ceiling. According to the president of the C. C. Club, the stairs are made of Italian marble.

Plate 6.11. Ballroom, C. C. Club, Herrin
While community residents used the room frequently, the paramount celebration came on Columbus Day.

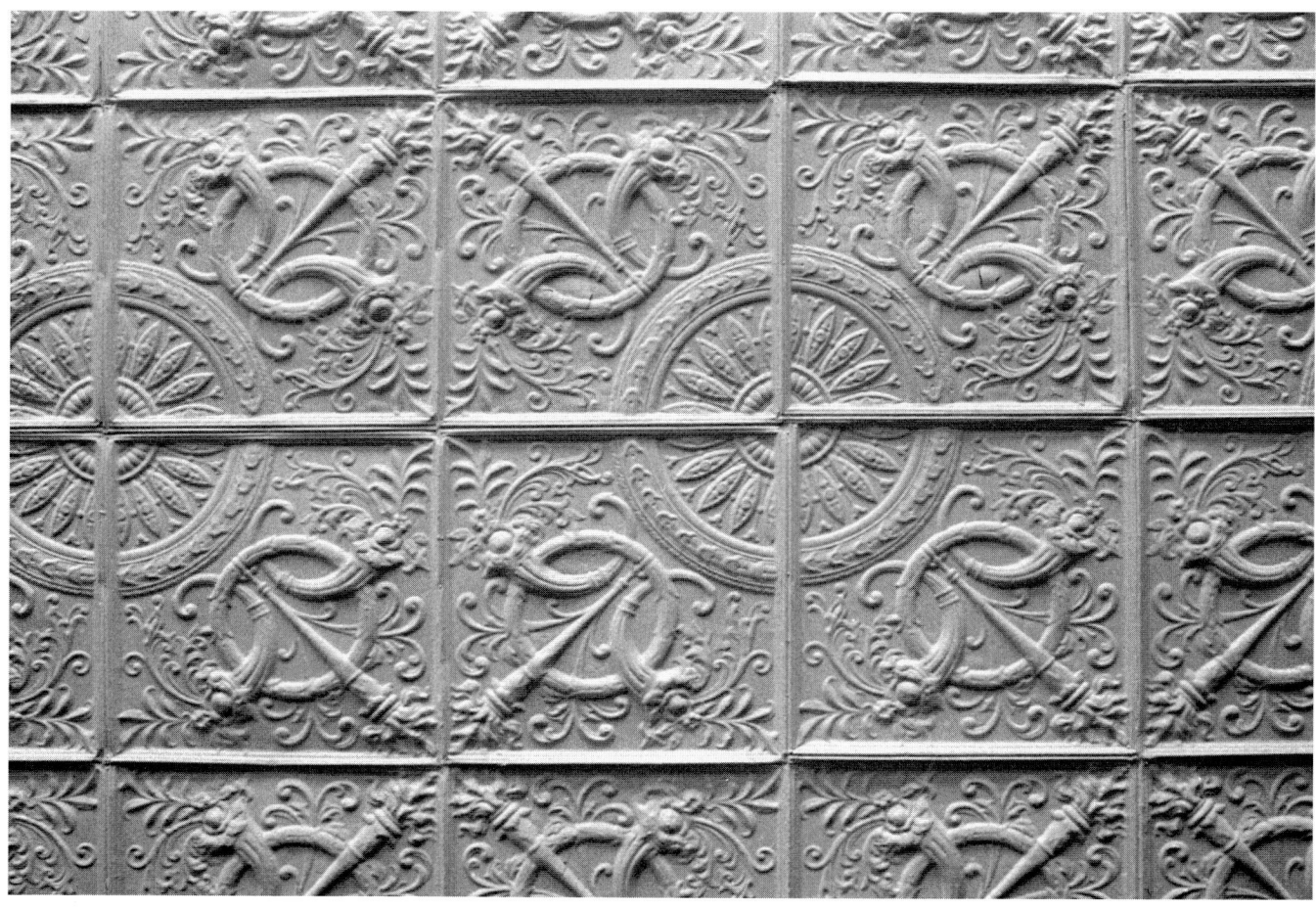

Plate 6.12. Detail of Ballroom Ceiling, C. C. Club, Herrin
Many fraternal organizations could order their organization's logo embossed in the pressed tin ceiling panels. This design, however, appears to be purely decorative.

Plate 6.13. Ballroom Bandstand, C. C. Club, Herrin
Dances were held here every Saturday night, but on Columbus Day the dancing commenced early in the morning and continued far into the night.

Plate 6.14. Town Bakery, Herrin
Originally called Moroni's, the store was once one of several Italian bakeries in Herrin. Built in 1911, the bakery uses a brick oven constructed by Italian immigrants and still makes Italian baked goods from traditional recipes.

Plate 6.15. Display Window, Town Bakery, Herrin
The window features antique baking implements formerly used in the business.

Plate 6.16. Detail of Facade, Dell'Era Building, Herrin
A close-up of this building shows elaborate ornamental brickwork. This commercial building was constructed c. 1911 by the prominent Italian businessman Louis Dell'Era, who also platted a mining town in his name. The town "Dell'Era" disappeared after the mine closed.

Plate 6.17. Northside Neighborhood, Herrin
Described as a "Lombardy neighborhood" by residents, typical Italian homes had gardens. "Everybody had a garden," both vegetable and flower, a homeowner recalled.

Plate 6.18. Grape Arbor, "Lombardy Neighborhood," Herrin
"Everybody made wine in Italy, and everybody's got a grape arbor," Angelo Calcaterra recalled. "My dad had a grape arbor in the back. We always had a bottle of wine on the table when we'd eat."

7. The Slovakians

Perhaps the single most vital factor uniting the Slovakian immigrants has been their faith. Linking groups from a diversity of regions in east-central Europe, the Orthodox Christian religion formed a cohesive bond in the Old Country. That faith was transferred intact to southern Illinois. Residents have vividly narrated tales from their own or their parents' pasts, describing flights from the decaying Austro-Hungarian Empire. The regions from which they came today lie in extreme southeastern Poland, eastern Slovakia, and the western part of the Soviet Ukraine. Some sought to escape extreme poverty; others hoped to elude years of compulsory military service. Still others desired a new life in America, and the prosperous soft coal mines in southern Illinois provided employment opportunities. Many immigrants entered during the first two decades of the twentieth century. Selecting booming coal towns like Royalton, Dowell, and Colp, the immigrants established a physical and cultural presence still felt today.

Opportunities for the immigrants to reshape the physical landscape were fewer than perhaps with any other group previously discussed. By the 1920s the area had been long settled, thus providing few areas to homestead and transform. Moreover, mass production of houses and home plans virtually eliminated the possibility of ethnic structures by restricting building materials and presenting national popular styles for emulation. In addition, by the 1920s native American pride and xenophobia mitigated even minor landscape modifications like renaming cities or streets.

Nevertheless, this new group also stamped its mark on the landscape. Prosperous coalfields needed workers who required housing. The companies readily obliged. Almost overnight, company towns serviced by company stores blossomed at Dowell and Colp, while a new neighborhood arose in Royalton. The houses, constructed by the coal companies and rented (or sold) to workers, created carbon-copy neighborhoods where the houses looked precisely the same. To introduce individuality and maintain personality, the newcomers remodeled their environments to resemble as much as possible those they had left behind. Fences enclosed yards, which became small pastures for cows, pigs, and chickens. Sheds protected livestock and tools. Gardens provided extra food for impoverished miners' families. Particularly in the smaller towns, according to one resident, the newcomers "always stuck with their own people and just didn't want to mingle with nobody else." Thus, specific neighborhoods comprised a welcome nucleus of compatriots. For example, Dowell had a "Dago Hill" and a "Budapest," and Royalton had a "Russian Row." Even nondescript buildings took on an ethnic character when they became specifically identified with the Slovakian group. Selected stores featured authentic Slovakian foods, or specific taverns provided traditional music for Old Country dances.

Most crucial, however, was their faith. In new towns and in Slovakian neighborhoods, an Orthodox Christian church anchored the community and its residents. "The first thing they would do was build a church," a woman recalled. Inside those sacred walls, services in the language of past generations preserved cultural traditions. Ethnic antagonism, both real and feared, reinforced cultural differences and enhanced group unity. Both processes influenced the cultural landscape by guaranteeing Slovakian culture would persist in southern Illinois.

In the communities, various Slavic dialects persisted vigorously on the streets and in the churches. Families traditionally celebrated Christmas on January 7 ("Old Christmas"), avoiding Anglo-American commercialism but demarcating them as different from Roman Catholic and Protestant neighbors. Mothers passed to daughters housekeeping skills such as embroidery and sewing. Even though sons attended school and thus acquired greater English proficiency and knowledge of American culture, families arranged many marriages, and wedding celebrations lasted for days of singing, dancing, feasting, and imbibing. In general, older residents recall a time when village life in southern Illinois strongly resembled, both physically and culturally, village life in eastern Europe.

For most of the area's Slovakian communities, life remained similar to this until about twenty years ago. By that time, social forces had begun to modify the physical and cultural characteristics of the Slovakian-Americans. Prosperity left the coalfields for other areas. The Orthodox chapel in Dowell closed, the company businesses collapsed, and residents abandoned homes. Mild antagonism persisted toward the "Russian Communist" church, and thus some parishioners surrendered their second language or church affiliation.

Nevertheless, the church in Royalton still proudly provides a physical foundation upon which to maintain cultural traditions. Christmas has been moved to December 25 ("New Christmas"), but parishioners still follow Easter customs and bring baskets for blessing, filled with traditionally decorated eggs and specially prepared foods. Slovakian dialects, mixed with English words, may occasionally be heard at church activities when older women cooperate in cooking foods. Many families perpetuate Old Country recipes, especially at parish social functions. Very rarely now are folk dances performed at these events. Still, on tombstones, in church, and in private homes, religious symbols reinforce the spiritual as well as the cultural bonds uniting the Slovakian-Americans today.

Like the other immigrants groups of southern Illinois, the Slovakians made a conspicuous impact on the physical and cultural landscape. But, like other groups, perhaps their greatest impact lies in the generations of area residents who benefited, materially and spiritually, from the hardships of the first generation. As one resident proudly stated: "My father came from the foreign country. He always made the remark, 'I had a rough time. I didn't have much of a chance, so I'm going to see to it that my children do.' So he sacrificed a lot. He worked hard all of his life, worked in the coal mine." By doing so his parent, and many others, physically and culturally shaped the Slovakian-American communities of southern Illinois.

Plate 7.1. Protection of the Virgin Mary Orthodox Church, Royalton
Parishioners began the building in 1914 and completed it by 1918. The building had no pews until 1964. Benches lined the walls for older parishioners, while the rest stood. The characteristic onion-shaped dome is typical of Byzantine architecture, especially that found in Slavic-speaking regions in Europe. Note the distinctive three-bar crosses atop the steeple and above the door; the bars represent the nameplate, crossbeam, and footrest of Jesus' cross. The parish hall stands to the left.

Plate 7.2. Protection of the Virgin Mary Orthodox Church, Royalton
Note the small dimensions of the church, indicative of the congregation's size. Parishioners estimate that Orthodox Christians comprise about 5 percent of Royalton's and Dowell's populations. The parishioners' original church had been in Muddy, Illinois. The present building has been built on the same plans, "only the church in Royalton is a little bigger," one resident felt.

Plate 7.3. Dedicatory Monument, Protection of the Virgin Mary Orthodox Church, Royalton
As is characteristic of all Orthodox churches, a monument was erected to commemorate this church's dedication. The inscription indicates the date of dedication. The monument is partially obscured by a more recent grotto to Mary.

Plate 7.4. Interior, Protection of the Virgin Mary Orthodox Church, Royalton
Compare the relatively humble exterior with the ornate beauty of the interior. The overall construction recapitulates that found in every other Orthodox church, great or small. The *inconostasis*, covered with icons, separates the congregation from the sacristy, symbolizing the division between sacred and secular. Photo by John M. Coggeshall.

Plate 7.5. Orthodox Christian Cemetery, Royalton Vicinity
Note the three-bar crosses atop or on many of the tombstones. In the foreground lies a row of stones marking the graves of Orthodox miners killed in an October 1914 mining disaster.

Plate 7.6. Tombstone, Orthodox Christian Cemetery, Royalton Vicinity

The stone marks the grave of a parishioner killed in a mining disaster near Royalton on 27 October, 1914. Photo by John M. Coggeshall.

Plate 7.7. United Mine Workers of America Union Hall, Royalton
The expansiveness of the building indicates the prominence which mining at one time held in the community. This view of the abandoned hall shows the annex, a large meeting room. Note "UMWA 1782" inlaid with tile on the decorative banding on the front of the building.

Plate 7.8. United Mine Workers of America Union Hall, Royalton
Now abandoned, the hall sits on the main street of town, denoting the former importance of mining for the community. The hall lies on the north end of town near the abandoned coal mine.

Plate 7.9. Main Thoroughfare, Royalton
Some buildings in the commercial district were abandoned or destroyed as the local coal-based economy declined. For example, the Bank of Royalton occupied the empty lot to the right of the photo as recently as fall 1985. Several blocks to the right is the Orthodox neighborhood, nicknamed "Russian Row" by non-Slovakian residents.

Plate 7.10. Dowell Mining Company Store, Dowell
A company store served almost every mining community. Prior to the Depression, when the mines operated at capacity, Dowell had several other businesses, a bank, and six taverns. One resident recalled how people would use scrip money. "The mine company paid in scrip, and they could go to the company store and buy clothing, or food, whatever they wanted." The company store is now abandoned.

Plate 7.11. Private Home, Dowell
Photo taken prior to World War II. "My father built this house," the occupant noted, "by saving money. We never bought anything on credit." As a child, she recalled that the house had a front and a back porch and two main entrances. In the fenced yard stood a cow shed, chicken coop, coal shed, and toolshed.

Plate 7.12. Private Home, Dowell
Same house as in prior photo. The house burned about twenty years ago, and the interior has been completely remodeled. Note that the front porch has been enclosed and the double entryway converted to a single entrance. The fence still encircles the property.

Plate 7.13. Azeling House, Royalton
Near the Orthodox church, the house sits in the "Russian Row" neighborhood and was built by the occupant's father around World War I. "We all tried to live in this area because we all belong to the church here," she explained. Typically, in the past these houses had outbuildings, farm animals, and a garden, all enclosed by a fence. "You could always tell foreign people because they had fences around their yards," she added.

Plate 7.14. Orthodox Chapel, Dowell
Note the vertical pole on the steeple with slots for the three bars of an Eastern Orthodox Christian cross. Closed for the past twenty years, the chapel served parishioners in a fairly large community. As was customary, the church's congregation stood during the services, men on the right and women on the left, for there were no other furnishings inside.

Plate 7.15. Company Houses, Colp Vicinity
Now abandoned, the homes had been associated with a community called Madison #9, after the adjacent mine. A pyramidal roof with a single chimney and double pen (two-room) construction seem to be common characteristics of workers' homes in southern Illinois mining communities. Herrin resident Angelo Calcaterra recalled, "Most of the people were under the domination of the mining company. If you bought a company house the prices were twice higher than any place else. You know, if you go to a company store and live in a company house, hell, you're lost. You'll never get out of it."

8. Eclectic Influences

Very few domestic structures remain unaltered through time. Repairs, alterations, and renovations are made to such structures on a regular basis. By the late 1800s many of the structures built by immigrants who had arrived in the mid-1800s or earlier had changed considerably. Traditional home places had undergone major renovations, usually in the form of additions, to accommodate the needs of growing families, with wings or even second floors added to the original house form. Alterations were also made to the exteriors of homes in an attempt to update appearances, such as the addition or removal of porches, windows, and doors.

Materials required to do these renovations were generally purchased from local hardware stores and lumberyards which stocked the latest products brought by railroad; thus the reliance upon locally available materials diminished. Whatever the impetus for the alteration of a structure, such activities usually changed the original form of the house or obscured the materials used in its construction, or both.

As communities and their surrounding areas became more established and segments of the society more prosperous, the desire to construct new homes in high style architectural forms currently in fashion surpassed the adherence to traditional architectural forms. Architectural styles fashionable in urban areas filtered into rural America, and a community's wealthier members—its doctors, lawyers, successful merchants, and farmers—sought plans for the construction of homes in Queen Anne, Victorian, or Italianate styles, just to name a few. In the late 1870s farm journals carried many articles exhorting farmers to transform original homesteads into examples of Victorian style, which would thus reflect families' desires to establish order and civilized values even on the far-flung prairies.

Not every family could afford to construct a high style home, but one could embellish an existing structure with fashionable details such as Queen Anne trimwork on eaves, gables, and porches or one could add porches with classical columns in Greek Revival style.

By the turn of the century, what is termed "popular architecture" had taken its place in American society. Most prospective home builders depended upon commercial pattern books for inspiration with regard to current architectural styles. A wide variety of materials was available on order for both exterior and interior construction. Most homes and public buildings became expressions of a style or a combination of styles currently in vogue, and adherence to ethnically influenced styles of building or land usage was largely abandoned. By the early twentieth century, an individual's choice of an architectural style was more contingent on a new Sears Roebuck catalog than Old Country traditions. Vernacular architecture had taken its place in mainstream American popular culture.

Plate 8.1. Hamilton House, Murphysboro
Built in 1867, the house is representative of Carpenter Gothic architectural style, characterized by steep pitched gabled roofs and gables embellished with ornamental vergeboards. Photo courtesy of Mike Jones, Murphysboro.

Plate 8.2. Halliday House, Cairo
Italianate structure was built c. 1868. The exterior walls are constructed from locally made brick; the interior features a staircase of wild cherry. Bought by Edwin Halliday, a riverboat worker, in 1872.

Plate 8.3. Steyer-Billington House, Golconda
Theodore Steyer, a prominent German businessman, constructed this Victorian-Italianate home c. 1870. The house has a T-shaped floor plan and features a prominent central tower that is clearly delineated from foundation to roof. Photo by Guy G. Weaver.

Plate 8.4. Sloan House, Golconda
In 1882 Judge Sloan built this Victorian-Italianate home on a bluff overlooking the town of Golconda. The tower features a mansard roof with decorative ironwork and arched-top windows at the third-floor level. Arched windows are a characteristic feature of Italianate homes. Photo courtesy of Lewis and Mabel Stannard, Golconda.

Plate 8.5. Stone Outbuilding, Sloan House, Golconda
This building predates the Civil War and may have been used in connection with the wine industry that once flourished in the area. Photo courtesy of Lewis and Mabel Stannard, Golconda.

Plate 8.6. Cloud State Bank and McCoy Memorial Library, McLeansboro
The bank building, completed in 1882, was designed by Chalon Cloud, its owner, in Second Empire style. McCoy Library was built in 1883–84 as a residence for Cloud's daughter. When she died, the building was willed to the city as a library. Photo by Guy G. Weaver.

Plate 8.7. Residence, Golconda
Historical photo of rural homestead embellished with fashionable Queen Anne trimwork on gables and porch; its large front parlor window surrounded by smaller, paned windows is also in Queen Anne style. Photo courtesy of Pope County Historical Society, Golconda.

Plate 8.8. Nelson House, Grand Tower
This cottage features Queen Anne styling in its diminutive proportions (approximately eighteen feet square) and patterned fringe at the eave. The square projecting bay window is typical of Carpenter Gothic styling. Note also the pyramidal roof and the hipped dormer window.

Plate 8.9. Christen Rubenacher House, Piopolis
Turn-of-the-century construction features concave mansard roof with wall dormers (windows extending into the roofline). Basic I-house form with vernacular Federalist styling.

Plate 8.10. Lohr Bottling Company, Cairo
Detail of main entrance to a once-thriving, German-owned enterprise established in 1901 but now closed. Photo by Guy G. Weaver.

Plate 8.11. Spalt's Barn, Cobden
Built c. 1907, this barn is constructed with pegs and has a stone foundation. The large windows rimmed with Pennsylvania Dutch designs are recent additions to the original structure.

Plate 8.12. Warner Wall House, Mound City
The house was built in 1913. Note the classical elaboration upon the basic house form, including the use of columns, a pediment on the front porch entry, and pedimented gables facing out of the cardinal axes of the house, typical of turn-of-the-century Queen Anne styling. Plans for the house were borrowed from the owner of an identical house in Hot Springs, Arkansas. Photo by Guy G. Weaver.

Plate 8.13. Tin Store Fronts, Mounds
Pressed metal storefronts feature a half-sunflower pattern, a prevalent motif of Queen Anne and Eastlake styles. The ornate colonnettes are fashioned from bent sheet metal and are hollow. Photo by Guy G. Weaver.

Plate 8.14. Downtown Businesses, Cairo
Known as "boomtown" storefronts, facades of embossed metal or cast iron could be ordered from catalogs and installed by local labor at minimal cost.

Plate 8.15. Barn and Silos, Benton Vicinity
Twin silos constructed of glazed tile. A staircase was built into the wooden structure that joins the two silos to provide access to each of them.

Plate 8.16. Shotgun Houses, Cairo
The shotgun house is a hybrid that developed in the West Indies and entered the United States in the early nineteenth century with the migration of Haitian Creoles to New Orleans. Shotgun houses derive from a fusion of Caribbean Indian, African, and European architectural components.

Plate 8.17. Shotgun Houses, Mounds
The common shotgun house type is one story, one room wide, and one to three (or more) rooms deep, with the main entrance in the front-facing gable end. Shotgun houses invariably have front porches and often possess vernacular embellishments such as the Queen Anne ornamentation seen on the corner house. Photo by Guy G. Weaver.

John M. Coggeshall, a Boston native, was raised in the Midwest, first in Webster Groves, Missouri, and then in Belleville, Illinois. Coggeshall received a master of arts degree in Ozark folklore from Southern Illinois University, Edwardsville, and a Ph.D. in anthropology from Southern Illinois University, Carbondale. Currently he serves as an assistant professor of anthropology at Clemson University.

Jo Anne Nast is a native of southern Illinois. She received her master of arts degree in anthropology from Southern Illinois University, Carbondale. She has worked with the Illinois State Historical Library and Society as School Services Supervisor, and she was editor of *Illinois History*. Nast is currently Curator of History at the University Museum, Southern Illinois University, Carbondale.

Randy Tindall was born in northwest Iowa and grew up on a farm near the town of Graettinger. He graduated from Southern Illinois University, Carbondale, with a degree in biological sciences. Following a tour as a Peace Corps volunteer, Tindall returned to Southern Illinois University to complete a master's degree in anthropology; he is currently pursuing his doctorate. Tindall has photographed and written for several organizations, including the United States Department of Agriculture.

 *Shawnee Books*

Also in this series

Foothold on a Hillside: Memories of a Southern Illinoisan
Charless Caraway

A Nickel's Worth of Skim Milk: A Boy's View of the Great Depression
Robert J. Hastings

A Penny's Worth of Minced Ham: Another Look at the Great Depression
Robert J. Hastings

Fishing Southern Illinois
Art Reid

The Music Came First: The Memoirs of Theodore Paschedag
Theodore Paschedag and Thomas J. Hatton